GREEK

& MIDDLE EASTERN COOKERY

Food Editor Donna Hay

BayBooks
An imprint of HarperCollins*Publishers*

CONTENTS

A BAY BOOKS PUBLICATION
An imprint of HarperCollinsPublishers

First published in 1992 in Australia by Bay Books, of
CollinsAngus&Robertson Publishers Pty Limited (ACN 009 913 517)
A division of HarperCollinsPublishers (Australia) Pty Limited
25 Ryde Road, Pymble NSW 2073, Australia

HarperCollinsPublishers (New Zealand) Limited
31 View Road, Glenfield, Auckland 10, New Zealand

HarperCollinsPublishers Limited
77-85 Fulham Palace Road, London W6 8JB, United Kingdom

Copyright © Bay Books 1992

National Library of Australia
Cataloguing-in-Publication data:

  Hay, Donna.
    Greek and Middle Eastern Cookery
    Includes index

    ISBN 1 86378 062 9.

    1. Cookery, Middle Eastern. 2. Cookery, Greek. I. Title.
    (Series: Bay Books cookery collection)

    641.5956

Front cover and chapter opener photography by Rowan Fotheringham
with styling by Donna Hay
(Spicy Algerian Sardines, recipe on page 29;
Tomato Roasted Octopus, recipe on page 29;
plates supplied by Corso de'Fiori, Darlinghurst)
Printed in Australia by Griffin Press, Adelaide

5 4 3 2 1
96 95 94 93 92

Along the Bosphorous, Istanbul

GREEK &
MIDDLE EASTERN COOKERY

The food from Greece and Middle Eastern countries is superb. The distinct delicious flavour combinations and interesting ingredients are combined imaginatively to give a sumptuous cuisine. Most of the ingredients used are widely available or can be found in specialty shops and delicatessens, particularly where there are communities from these areas.

Some of the food preservation techniques we use today came from the early settlers of the Middle Eastern regions. Fish was dried and salted in Egypt so it could be transported to distant places, olives were crushed to provide oil for cooking, lighting and heating, and many spices were dried. In Iran, roses were distilled to make rose water and this flavouring is still commonly used to flavour desserts in the Middle East. After the introduction of oranges from China, orange blossom water was also distilled.

The modern cuisine of the Middle East continues to reflect past traditions as well as the influence of the prevailing religion, Islam. Many dishes have adapted Persian styles of preparing and cooking food.

The Koran forbids the eating of pork. It advocates the eating of pure milk, grapes, pomegranates, dates, honey and figs, all of which are still eaten today.

Lamb and mutton are the most common meats eaten, with lamb fillets being used for kebabs, while tougher cuts are minced. Beef is now becoming more widely used. Both seafood and meat are often cooked over coals.

Nuts, such as pine nuts, almonds, pistachio nuts and hazelnuts, are very popular in Greek and Middle Eastern cooking, they feature in savoury and sweet dishes. One of the important uses of nuts is as a thickening for sauces.

A dish of sweetmeats combining fresh or dried dates with nuts such as almonds can be traced back to the nomadic Bedouins. Today this type of sweetmeat makes an excellent accompaniment to the thick, sweet Arabic coffee. Pistachio nuts are thought to be native to Iran and, with almonds, are mentioned in the Bible. Iranians use pistachio nuts in their baklava. The Arabs are also responsible for marzipan and nougat — two sweetmeats featuring almonds.

Vegetables are used extensively in Middle Eastern cuisine, including unusual vegetables such as okra. Eggplant is a favourite of Turkish, Lebanese and Greek dishes; it is made into a dip (baba ghanoush), stuffed with tomatoes and onions (and anchovies in Greece), used in the well-known moussaka or simply fried. Stuffing is a very popular method of serving vegetables and fruit throughout Greece and the Middle Eastern region.

The combination of fruit and meat is a specialty of Iranian cooking and dates back to ancient time. The Iranians stuff apples and quinces with a minced lamb mixture, serve a dried fruit and meat soup, and their sauces often combine fruits, either fresh or dried, with meat.

Commonly used spices include saffron, cinnamon, nutmeg and cumin. Popular herbs include chives, mint, tarragon, chervil, dill, coriander and bay leaves. Dried mint is often fried in a little ghee and poured over a dish just before serving.

Generally, olive oil or ghee are used for cooking throughout the region. Butter and other oils such as peanut oil can be substituted.

THE GREEK
& MIDDLE EASTERN
KITCHEN

Some useful equipment for cooking Middle Eastern and Greek dishes include a mortar and pestle to grind your own spices and nuts. In the Middle East, mortar and pestle are also used to grind meat for kibbeh.

A food processor is very handy, especially for the preparation of various dips, and also for kibbeh.

BREAD Pita, or pocket bread is popular in the Middle East and is eaten at every meal, particularly for scooping up softer foods such as dips and salads. It is used to make Middle Eastern style 'sandwiches', for example a falafel roll, which is pita bread wrapped around falafel, hummus (chick pea dip) and tabbouli salad. It is also useful at the end of the meal to mop up sauces.

Pide, a flat but more flaky bread, is used widely in Turkish cuisine. Pide with various fillings ('Turkish pizza') is one of the most popular dishes to be found in Turkish restaurants.

Pita bread and other Middle Eastern flat breads, available in many shapes and sizes, can be purchased in supermarkets. Freshly baked flat bread can be bought in Greek and Middle Eastern specialty stores and takeaway shops.

Flat bread becomes dry and hard very quickly but it can be easily revitalised by sprinkling with water and then warming it under the grill or oven. To heat a lot of bread before a meal, wrap it in foil and keep in the oven at a low heat.

Pita bread can be frozen but should be very fresh when put in the freezer. It can be heated in the oven or grill, straight from the freezer.

BURGHUL Cracked wheat is known as burghul, burghoul or bulgur and features in dishes such as tabbouli and kibbeh. After the wheat is harvested, the grains are washed then sorted. Next they are cooked until they split, then drained and dried. When the cracked wheat is dried it is ground to three consistencies: fine, medium or coarse. For the recipes in this book, use medium burghul, unless otherwise specified.

To prepare: Take the required amount of burghul, place in a bowl, cover with water and leave for 10 minutes. Drain well and press out excess water using the back of a spoon. For some recipes burghul needs to be dry. Spread out on absorbent paper and leave to dry, stirring occasionally.

CHEESE Feta is the most widely used cheese in Greek dishes, and is ideal for salads and pies. It can be bought either soft or hard.

Goat's cheese is popular in the Middle East and is delicious baked with herbs.

COFFEE Turkish coffee is renowned for being thick and strong. It is a perfect accompaniment to traditional sweetmeats. To maximise the flavour of coffee, place in a tightly sealed plastic bag and store in the freezer. It does not freeze solid and can be easily measured out when required. If you use a lot of coffee, purchase whole beans and grind them as needed.

In Greece and the Middle East, coffee is consumed in vast quantities at any hour of the day or night and is always accompanied by a glass of water.

Greek, Lebanese and Turkish coffee are all similar in taste and texture — the name varies according to where you are drinking it! The flavour is best if the coffee is prepared in a special copper coffee pot, which can be bought in Greek or Middle Eastern specialty stores. The coffee can also be successfully prepared in a saucepan kept for the purpose.

Buy Turkish or Mocca coffee beans in a coffee shop and grind them very finely. Place 1 heaped teaspoon of coffee and 1 heaped teaspoon of sugar per person into the pot. Cover with ½ cup (125 ml) cold water per person. Bring slowly to the boil. When foam rises, remove from heat and stir. Repeat this process twice but do not stir the last time. Sprinkle with cold water to allow the grounds to settle and pour into small cups. Do not drink the sediment. You may like to read your fortune from the sediment as they do in Greece!

FILO PASTRY Filo pastry, also spelt 'phyllo' or 'fillo', translates from the Arabic as 'leaves'. Although it is possible to make your own filo, the prepared commercial pastry is an excellent choice and much more convenient. It is extremely fragile and must be handled with care. Always buy filo that has a fairly advanced use-by date and store in the refrigerator, it does not need to be frozen. Once the packet has been opened, reseal filo in a clean plastic bag and return to the refrigerator. If filo pastry dries out during storage it will usually be only at the ends; just cut off the dry bits and use the rest.

To use filo, take three clean tea-towels. Place one flat on the work surface. Wet another, then squeeze it as dry as possible. Open the pastry, unroll and place on the dry tea-towel. Cover with the other dry towel, then the damp one. The pastry is now ready to use but must always be kept covered to prevent drying out. If the top towel becomes too dry, moisten and squeeze again. Never place the damp towel directly on the pastry because it will turn to a soft dough and become unusable.

FLAVOURED WATER Rose water and orange blossom water can be purchased from Lebanese or other Middle Eastern stores or from chemists. The strength of rose water varies greatly so add only a few drops at first: an overpowering flavour will spoil a dish.

HERBS AND SPICES When buying dried herbs and spices, purchase them in quantities to suit your cooking needs. They should be stored in well-sealed containers and placed in dark, dry areas as their aroma and colour is rapidly lost when exposed to light. Even when properly stored, herbs and spices do not have an indefinite shelf life and any over two years old should be discarded because their original perfume will have faded. It is preferable to buy whole dried herbs and spices as opposed to ground as they last longer and can be freshly ground for each recipe.

Fresh herbs add a special flavour to many dishes. It is ideal to plant your own and have a fresh selection at hand whenever needed. Mint, coriander, parsley, chives and dill would be a good selection for your kitchen herb garden.

Choose fresh herbs that have bright, fresh leaves and are not starting to turn yellow and go to seed. To store, lightly sprinkle the leaves with water and stand them in a container of water.

NUTS Almonds, hazelnuts, pine nuts and walnuts are the nuts most commonly used in Middle Eastern cooking. Buy your nuts in the quantities you will use. Always buy almonds unpeeled because they keep better; the boiling water used when peeling the nuts helps to 'plump' and freshen them. Hazelnuts generally come unpeeled and must be roasted before peeling. To store nuts, place in sealed containers and store in the refrigerator.

To peel almonds, place them in a pan, cover with cold water and bring to the boil. Simmer for 1 minute, then drain and cool with cold water. The almonds should slip out of their skins.

A bread seller in Istanbul

To peel hazelnuts, spread them in a Swiss roll tin and place in a moderate oven 180°C (350°F). Roast for 10 minutes, or until the flesh starts to change colour. Tip onto a clean tea-towel, gather up the corners tightly and roll the bundle on a work surface. The skins should rub off.

Walnuts are generally not available peeled. However, for some recipes, particularly if the skins are bitter, it is best to peel them. Prepare as for almonds and after cooking, remove the skins, using a skewer for the folds.

PULSES OR LEGUMES These should be bought as fresh as possible. The cheapest way to buy pulses or legumes is loose; you can buy the exact amount needed and do not have to worry about storing or using the excess. Canned pulses save a lot of time and reduce fuel costs, but for a long-cooked dish, use the dried version.

Chick peas are widely used and are found in well-known dishes such as hummus and falafel. Wash chick peas first in water. Always soak them before cooking: cover with cold water and leave for at least three hours. Top up with cold water as necessary. Remove any peas that float. To speed up the soaking process, after washing the peas cover them with boiling water and leave for one hour before cooking.

Chick peas can be peeled either before or after cooking. Before cooking and after the peas have soaked, work them between thumb and index finger to loosen the skin, returning the peeled peas to the soaking liquid. Another method is

to roughly dry the chick peas and place in a tea-towel. Wrap them up and work the towel back and forth on a work surface until the skins are loosened. The skins are much easier to remove after cooking; cool the peas and simply slip the skins off.

To cook chick peas, place them in a pan and cover with fresh water. Bring to the boil, cover and simmer until tender, 1½ to 2½ hours. Skim the surface occasionally and top up the water level. Small peeled onions and a bay leaf may be added to the cooking pot. When the peas are tender, drain and use as desired.

Canned chick peas are useful because you can eliminate the soaking and cooking stages. They are sometimes labelled garbanzos, which is their Spanish name. Canned peas are not suitable for falafel.

Split peas are either yellow or green and need no soaking before cooking. They will take about 1½ hours to cook. Cover and simmer without stirring for about an hour, then test.

When cooking pulses, do not add salt until they are cooked.

RICE Basmati rice is a fragrant rice grown in Pakistan and is used in many Middle Eastern dishes. It is available in supermarkets.

To prepare basmati, wash it at least five times or until the water runs clear. Pick out and discard any husks or discoloured grains.

Some recipes specify basmati rice. There is no substitute for the flavour of basmati; other rices can be used but the flavour and aroma will be different.

Usually long grain rice is favoured for dishes, though short grain is

better for stuffing vegetables. Long grain rice is easier to cook as it remains tender, firm, separate and fluffy, if cooked properly.

Rice is cooked in different ways throughout the Middle East. In Lebanon, water is boiled with some butter and salt and the rice then cooked by the absorption method.

In Syria, the rice is cooked in boiling salted water and then mixed with melted butter.

Iranian (chilau) rice is made by cooking presoaked rice on a high heat for about 8 minutes, then the rice is transferred to a pan with melted butter in it and is cooked over a low heat for 15 to 20 minutes. A crust will form on the bottom which is delicious.

The Egyptian method is to sauté the rice grains in butter or oil until translucent and the grains are coated. Water is then added and the rice cooked over a low heat, undisturbed. Saffron can be added to the butter or oil, to make a yellow and deliciously aromatic rice.

Rice is often cooked with fresh herbs, such as chives, dill, parsley, tarragon and mint. The herbs should be thrown in when the rice is nearly cooked.

Another delicious way to serve rice is to sauté some nuts such as pine nuts, pistachios and almonds in some butter or oil and toss through prepared rice.

SAFFRON Saffron is a magnificent spice, with a subtle perfume and colour that makes any dish special. It is the dried stamens of a certain crocus and must be individually hand picked; this makes it very expensive because it takes many

thousands of stamens to weigh even 500 g. Spain produces most of the world's saffron.

Saffron should never be added directly to a dish because its colour and perfume must be extracted beforehand. Place the saffron threads in a small heatproof container and cover with a little boiling water; leave to cool, then lightly squeeze the threads. Add the threads and liquid to the dish.

Powdered saffron is available in small packets and is not as expensive. Only a small amount of the powder should be added: dishes quickly turn a deep orange if care is not taken.

Turmeric is not a substitute for saffron, its colour and flavour being completely different.

TAHINI Tahini paste is made from sesame seeds that are toasted and ground to a paste. It is available in cans or jars and should be stirred well before use because the oil separates when the paste is left to stand. Keep tahini covered and in the refrigerator once it has been opened.

To make your own tahini, dry-fry sesame seeds until they are just starting to turn colour; stir with a wooden spoon. Take from heat and keep stirring until cool. If seeds start burning, turn them into a

Harbour Rethimnon in Crete

A fruit market in Greece

bowl. Place seeds in a blender or food processor and process to a paste. Add a little oil as necessary. Store as above. There is no substitute for tahini.

VEGETABLES These are an integral part of Greek and Middle Eastern cooking. They do not fall in the category of side dish or accompaniment. They are served in dips, salads, stews, soups, pilafs and are stuffed, sautéed and steamed. Flavour, texture and colour are all important aspects of cooking vegetables in Greece and the Middle East. The most popular vegetables include zucchinis (courgettes), eggplants (aubergines), tomatoes, cucumbers, artichokes, okra, spinach, capsicum (peppers) and onions. The size and shape is important depending on how the vegetables are to be used. For instance, if zucchinis are to be stuffed, they should be large, but for casseroles they should be smaller.

Buy smallish eggplants for stuffing, and larger ones for casseroles and other dishes.

VINE LEAVES Vine leaves are available in packets, loose, or fresh if you grow your own grapes.

Packaged vine leaves are usually preserved in brine. Rinse them carefully in hot water, snip the stem and place, shiny side down, on a work surface. Loose leaves should be rinsed carefully, blanched in boiling water for 1 minute, then drained. Remove fresh leaves from the vine, and snip off the stalk. Wash very well, then blanch in boiling salted water 3 to 4 minutes.

No good substitution can be made for vine leaves. Other vegetable leaves such as soft-leaved lettuce, blanched, can be used but the taste and appearance will not be authentic.

YOGHURT Natural yoghurt is used in many Greek and Middle Eastern dishes, in soups, salads, meat and

vegetable dishes and desserts. It is generally known as laban and pasteurised, pasteurised/homogenised and skim milk are all suitable for making yoghurt.

Yoghurt cultures are destroyed at temperatures above 46°C and will not 'grow' at temperatures below 32°C. An electric yoghurt making machine is excellent if you prepare a lot of yoghurt at home. Follow the manufacturer's instructions.

A good quality commercial yoghurt is necessary as a starter; the home-made yoghurt can be used as a starter within three days.

HOW TO MAKE YOGHURT

4 cups (1 litre) milk
2 tablespoons natural yoghurt

1 Heat milk to scalding, almost boiling, remove from heat and cool to 40°C to 43°C. (If you do not have a thermometer, dip your finger in the milk and if it still feels hot after the count of 10 then it is at the correct temperature.)
2 Combine yoghurt with a little of the warm milk and stir into the milk. Pour into a bowl, cover with a plate and wrap in towels or blankets. Leave at room temperature, undisturbed, for 6 to 8 hours. If the mixture is jogged or stirred, the yoghurt will separate.
3 Once it has set, refrigerate for two hours before using. Store in a bowl or sterilised jars.

Variation: Skim milk can replace ordinary milk. Dissolve 3 tablespoons powdered skim milk in the skim milk before scalding. Continue as above.

MAKES ABOUT 4 CUPS (1 LITRE)

Starters

Soups are an important part of Mediterranean and Middle Eastern food. They often contain lentils and beans, and may be based on yoghurt, or rice as in *Egg and Lemon Soup*.

Appetisers, or *mezze*, are to the Middle East what Yum Cha is to the Chinese — an exciting combination of foods to whet the appetite.

When serving a mezze, offer a selection of at least three different dishes, choosing a dip, a vegetable dish or salad and one other recipe such as Kibbeh (this is in the meat chapter). Also, pass around flat bread such as pita, marinated olives, and nuts such as walnuts, almonds and pine nuts.

Turkish-style coffee or wine can be drunk with mezze.

In this chapter are traditional dishes such as *hummus* (chick pea dip), baba ghanoush (eggplant salad) and stuffed vine leaves, and many other favourites from the region.

Baked Goat Cheese and Marinated Capsicum

*Select clean jars with lids
and place in a large
saucepan. Cover with
water, bring to the boil
and simmer for
20 minutes. Drain and
invert on to a clean
tea-towel.*

MARINATED OLIVES WITH HERBS

400 g Kalamata olives or other black olives

6 coriander seeds

3 cloves garlic

4 to 6 sprigs thyme

2 bay leaves

olive oil

1 Wash olives well. Place them in a jar with coriander seeds, garlic, thyme and bay leaves. Cover with olive oil.

2 Seal and store in a cool dark place. When all the olives have been eaten the oil is flavoursome and can be used for salad dressings.

MAKES 500 ML

MARINATED CAPSICUM

4 red capsicum (peppers)

4 yellow capsicum (peppers)

2 tablespoons rosemary leaves

1 teaspoon coriander seeds

2 cups (500 ml) olive oil

1 Cut capsicum in half and remove seeds. Place under a preheated grill, cut side down. Grill until skins are black and blistered. Place capsicum inside a plastic bag, tie the top and set aside for 5 minutes to 'sweat' skins. Peel off skins.

2 Pack capsicum in a large jar with rosemary and coriander. Pour in oil and seal jar. Store in the refrigerator for up to 3 months. Serve with bread or in salads.

MAKES ABOUT 750 ML

PICKLED ARTICHOKE HEARTS

12 artichoke hearts

1 tablespoon fresh lemon juice

20 small oregano leaves

1 cup (250 ml) white wine

1 cup (250 ml) olive oil

1 Pack artichoke hearts in jars. Pour over lemon juice and sprinke with oregano leaves.

2 Fill with equal parts of wine and olive oil. Seal and store in a cool dark place for 4 to 6 weeks before serving.

MAKES 500 ML

⊹ **ARTICHOKE HEARTS**

It is recommended that you buy artichoke hearts packed in brine for pickling. These are available in both jars and cans in supermarkets.

PICKLED CHILLI PEPPERS

2 cups (500 ml) water

2 cups (500 ml) white vinegar

3 tablespoons salt

750 g mild green chilli peppers, washed and stalks trimmed

1 hot red chilli pepper for each jar used

1 clove garlic for each jar used (optional)

1 Combine water, vinegar and salt in a pan, bring to the boil and simmer for 1 minute. Place chillies in jars and cover with hot liquid.

2 Place one red chilli and, if desired, one clove garlic in each jar. With a skewer, burst any air bubbles in the jar. Seal and store for at least one week before using. Refrigerate after opening. The chillies can be drained and served in a little olive oil as part of a *mezze*.

MAKES 1 LITRE

Sauté onion and celery until lightly golden, then add drained lentils.

Purée lentils in a sieve, blender or food processor.

Combine the egg yolks in a bowl with a little hot sauce.

RED LENTIL SOUP

1 cup (200 g) red lentils

50 g butter

1 large onion, chopped

1 stalk celery, chopped

6 cups (1½ litres) water or chicken stock

salt and pepper

½ to 1 teaspoon paprika

1 teaspoon ground cumin (optional)

1 tablespoon plain flour

1 cup (250 ml) milk

2 egg yolks, beaten

fresh lemon juice

1 Wash lentils and discard any that float. Heat half the butter in a heavy-based pan. Sauté onion and celery until lightly golden.

2 Add drained lentils, stirring to coat with butter. Pour in 4 cups (1 litre) of liquid, salt and pepper to taste, paprika and cumin, if using. Bring to the boil, reduce heat and simmer until lentils are tender, skimming as necessary. Add any extra liquid as required.

3 Purée lentils in a food processor or push through a sieve, using the reserved liquid if necessary. Return to pan.

4 In a separate saucepan, melt remaining butter, add flour and cook for 1 minute. Gradually add milk and bring to the boil, stirring constantly. Simmer for a few minutes. Season to taste.

5 Add a little hot white sauce to egg yolks, combine well and return to sauce. Stir sauce into lentil purée and gently heat. Add lemon juice to taste. Serve hot.

SERVES 4 TO 6

QUINCE SOUP

300 g lamb, trimmed and diced

2 onions, finely chopped

⅓ cup (60 g) chick peas, soaked (optional)

½ teaspoon freshly ground black pepper

60 g butter

2 quinces, peeled, seeded and diced

½ teaspoon ground turmeric

½ teaspoon ground cinnamon

juice 1 lemon

sugar

1 Place lamb pieces, onions, chick peas and pepper in a pan. Add water to cover and bring to the boil. Reduce heat and simmer for 1½ hours, skimming occasionally.

2 Melt butter and sauté quinces for 10 minutes. Add turmeric and cinnamon and cook for 1 minute. Add to soup and simmer for a further 50 minutes or until quinces and chick peas are tender. Add lemon juice and sugar to taste. Serve hot.

SERVES 4 TO 6

Red Lentil Soup

✥ QUINCES

The quince was known in Greece in the time of Homer. It was sacred to Aphrodite, the goddess of love.

Quinces are generally eaten cooked. They turn pink during the cooking process. Quinces are perfect for stewed dishes.

Yoghurt is the anglicised Turkish word for fermented milk. If you buy it instead of making your own, make sure that it is made with live bacterial cultures. Some commercial brands use chemicals to make milk 'seem' like yoghurt, having none of the beneficial qualities of 'live' yoghurt.

CHILLED YOGHURT SOUP

2 large cucumbers
4 cups (1 litre) natural yoghurt
½ cup (125 ml) chilled water
1 teaspoon white pepper
½ cup fresh, finely chopped mint
spring onions, finely chopped
crushed ice or ice blocks

1 Wash and dry cucumbers, then top and tail. Peel them leaving green stripes. Halve lengthways, scoop out and discard seeds. Halve lengthways again and slice finely.
2 Pour yoghurt into a bowl and stir well until smooth. Add chilled water gradually to thin until you achieve desired consistency. Add cucumbers, and season to taste with pepper. Chill for several hours.
3 To serve, stir through mint and spring onions. Place some crushed ice or an ice block in individual serving dishes and pour in soup.

SERVES 4

EGG AND LEMON SOUP

8 cups (2 litres) chicken stock
¾ cup (155 g) rice
3 eggs
¼ cup (60 ml) fresh lemon juice
freshly ground black pepper

1 Heat chicken stock in a large pan. Add rice and cook for 15 minutes or until soft.
2 Beat eggs in a bowl until frothy. Gradually add lemon juice and continue beating. Slowly add 1 cup (250 ml) of stock to eggs, beating well.
3 Add egg mixture to remaining stock and stir over low heat for 1 minute. Serve with pepper and fresh crusty bread.

SERVES 4 TO 6

CHICKEN SOUP WITH YOGHURT

4 cups (1 litre) chicken stock
¼ cup (60 g) rice
½ teaspoon freshly ground black pepper
1¼ cups (310 ml) natural yoghurt
3 egg yolks, lightly beaten
1 to 2 tablespoons chopped fresh mint

1 Bring stock to the boil in a pan. Add rice and pepper; cook until rice is tender.
2 Combine yoghurt and egg yolks.
3 When rice is cooked, combine 1 cup (250 ml) of the hot liquid with yoghurt. Gradually stir this mixture into soup and heat gently until soup thickens slightly. Serve garnished with fresh mint. If using dried mint, sauté it briefly in 15 g butter and spoon over soup before serving.

SERVES 4

CREAMY AVOCADO SOUP

2 large avocados
1½ tablespoons fresh lemon juice
40 g butter
⅓ cup (40 g) plain flour
2 cups (500 ml) milk
2 cups (500 ml) chicken stock
white pepper
paprika
1 lemon, sliced

1 Mash avocado flesh well in a bowl. Add lemon juice and combine.
2 Melt butter in a saucepan. Add flour and cook over a medium heat for 2 to 3 minutes, stirring constantly. Remove from heat. Gradually add milk and stock, stirring well. Bring to the boil, reduce heat and simmer for 5 minutes. Add white pepper to taste.
3 Combine avocado with 1 cup (250 ml) of hot liquid. Return to pan, simmer to heat avocado. Garnish with paprika and lemon.

SERVES 4

SPINACH AND LAMB SOUP

500 g lamb, trimmed and diced

lamb bones

6 cups (1½ litres) water

6 peppercorns

1 bay leaf

½ cup (90 g) rice

30 g butter

2 cloves garlic, crushed

1 large onion, finely chopped

1 bunch English spinach

1 Place meat and bones in a pan with water, peppercorns and bay leaf. Bring to the boil, reduce heat and simmer, partially covered, until lamb is tender, about 1 hour. When the meat is tender, remove, and discard bones. Add rice and continue cooking.

2 Heat butter and sauté garlic and onion until transparent. Add to soup.

3 Remove tougher spinach stalks, roll up leaves and shred finely. Add to soup and continue cooking until the rice and spinach are tender. Serve hot.

SERVES 4

✥ SOUP WITH RICE

Many of the Greek and Middle Eastern soups are based on rice. These thick hearty soups are meals in themselves especially if served with bread and salad.

Spinach and Lamb Soup

Turkish Wedding Soup

TURKISH WEDDING SOUP

500 g boneless lamb, trimmed and diced

⅓ cup (40 g) seasoned plain flour

3 tablespoons oil

6 cups (1.5 litres) water

1 marrow bone, cracked or lamb bones

1 onion, quartered

1 carrot, chopped

6 black peppercorns

2 egg yolks

2 tablespoons fresh lemon juice

45 g butter

3 teaspoons paprika

1 Roll meat pieces in seasoned flour. Heat oil in a large pan, add lamb in batches and cook until browned. Gradually add water, stirring well. Add marrow bone.

2 Bring to the boil, skimming as necessary. Add onion, carrot and peppercorns. Reduce heat and simmer partially covered for 1½ to 2 hours or until meat is tender. Skim occasionally. Remove meat and strain soup, discarding vegetables and bones. Return meat to soup and reheat.

3 Combine egg yolks with lemon juice in a bowl. Add 1 cup (250 ml) of hot liquid and beat well. Return to soup and cook over very gentle heat for 1 to 2 minutes. Remove from heat and cover to keep warm.

4 Melt butter in a small pan and add paprika. To serve, turn soup into a tureen and pour over butter and paprika. Alternatively, serve soup individually and spoon over a little of the butter mixture. Serve hot.

SERVES 4

TARAMASALATA

2 slices stale wholemeal bread, crusts removed

75 g smoked cod's roe

1 clove garlic, crushed

pinch cayenne pepper

juice 1 to 2 lemons

paprika

⅔ cup (160 ml) oil

1 Soak bread slices in a little water.

2 Remove skins from roe and pound to a smooth paste. Squeeze bread dry and add to roe with garlic and cayenne pepper. Continue to pound mixture until it is really smooth. Gradually stir in lemon juice and oil and beat vigorously. Alternatively, all ingredients can be put in a blender or food processor and blended until smooth.

3 Transfer to serving dish, sprinkle with paprika and serve with toast.

SERVES 2 TO 4

Roll trimmed pieces of meat in plain flour seasoned with salt and pepper.

Skim off any residue while bringing the mixture to the boil.

Combine egg yolks and lemon juice, then add 1 cup (250 ml) of hot liquid and beat well.

FALAFEL

¼ cup (45 g) fine burghul or ⅓ cup (60 g)
dried broad beans

2 cups (220 g) dried chick peas, soaked
overnight and peeled

2 to 3 cloves garlic, crushed

3 spring onions, finely chopped

½ teaspoon ground cumin

½ teaspoon ground coriander

1 tablespoon finely chopped fresh parsley

1 teaspoon baking powder

freshly ground black pepper

oil for deep frying

1 Cover burghul with hot water and soak
for 10 minutes. Drain and press out excess
water. Finely grind chick peas, using the fine
screen of a grinder, or a food processor.
Repeat if necessary; mixture should be
very fine.

2 Place chick pea mixture in a bowl with all
remaining ingredients except oil. Mix
thoroughly, cover and chill for 1 hour. Take
2 tablespoons of the mixture and, with wet
hands, shape it into patties. Set aside for
30 minutes.

3 Heat oil. Fry the falafel in batches until
golden brown and cooked through. Drain on
crumpled absorbent paper.

4 Serve as part of a mezze selection or as a
falafel sandwich. To make the sandwich,
spread a piece of flat bread with chick pea
dip (see page 18) or tahini, add a little
shredded lettuce and sliced tomato or
tabbouli, place two or three falafel on top
and squeeze a little lemon juice over. Roll
up tightly.

MAKES 12

EGGPLANT DIP
Baba Ghanoush

500 g eggplant (aubergine), halved

2 to 3 cloves garlic

salt

juice 2 to 3 lemons

⅓ cup (80 ml) tahini

1 Place eggplant cut side down under a
preheated grill, turning occasionally until
skin blisters and turns black, about
30 minutes. Alternatively, place on centre
rack of a preheated moderate oven 180°C
(350°F) until blistered. Peel, top and tail
eggplant while still hot. Roughly chop it
then purée using a mortar and pestle,
blender or food processor.

2 Crush garlic with salt and add to
eggplant with most of the lemon juice and
tahini. Beat or blend well until combined.
Adjust the flavour with remaining lemon
juice and tahini. Chill.

3 Serve in a shallow dish with flat bread.

SERVES 6 TO 8

Eggplant Dip

✦ TAHINI

*This is a paste made from
sesame seeds. It can be
bought in supermarkets
and health food stores.
Tahini is used extensively
in Middle Eastern
countries in dips and
sauces. It has a nutty
flavour and a texture
similar to that of smooth
peanut butter, and can be
used in the same way as
peanut butter. Store
opened jars of tahini in
the refrigerator and stir
thoroughly before using.*

Ready cooked canned chick peas can be purchased in supermarkets. Wash and drain these well before using. It is not recommended to use canned chick peas for falafel.

CHICK PEA DIP

Hummus

⅔ cup (125 g) dried chick peas, soaked overnight

2 cloves garlic, crushed

½ to ⅔ cup (125 to 160 ml) tahini

2 to 3 lemons

salt and freshly ground black pepper

paprika

sprigs fresh parsley

flat bread

1 Place chick peas in a pan and cover with water. Bring to the boil, cover and simmer until tender, 1½ to 2½ hours. Skim the surface occasionally and top up the water level. When tender, drain and reserve cooking liquid.

2 Blend chick peas in a food processor or push through a sieve, discarding any skins. Add reserved cooking liquid if necessary.

3 Add garlic, ½ cup (125 ml) tahini and juice of two lemons. Taste and add more tahini and lemon juice, if desired. Season to taste with salt and pepper.

Chick Pea Dip

4 Spoon into a serving dish. Smooth the top and sprinkle with paprika. Garnish with fresh parsley and serve with flat bread (pita).

SERVES 4 TO 6

FILO SPINACH FINGERS

Filo pastry is a tissue thin, pliable pastry made with high gluten white flour, oil, salt and water. Filo is a Greek word meaning 'leaf'.

2 bunches English spinach

1 tablespoon oil

1 onion, chopped

½ teaspoon ground nutmeg

½ teaspoon ground cinnamon

freshly ground black pepper

6 sheets filo pastry

½ cup (125 ml) oil

1 Preheat oven to 190°C (375°F). Remove centre stalks of spinach and wash leaves. Pack into a pan and cook, covered, over a gentle heat until softened. Drain well and chop; place in a bowl.

2 Heat oil in a pan and sauté onion until transparent. Add to spinach with nutmeg, cinnamon and pepper to taste. Beat well to combine.

3 Place pastry on a dry tea-towel and cut in half lengthways. Cover with another dry tea-towel and then a damp tea-towel. Take one sheet of pastry and brush with oil. Place two tablespoons of filling along short edge of pastry, 1 cm from the edge. Fold over ends and fold up sides. Roll to form a sausage shape. Brush with oil and place on a lightly greased baking tray. Repeat with the remaining pastry and filling. Bake for 20 minutes, or until golden and crisp. Serve warm.

MAKES 12

Crispy Fried Calamari

CHEESY PUFFS

6 sheets ready rolled puff pastry

1 egg, lightly beaten

CHEESE FILLING

60 g butter

⅓ cup (40 g) plain flour

1 cup (250 ml) milk

250 g feta cheese, crumbled

125 g Cheddar cheese, grated

2 eggs

½ teaspoon ground nutmeg

½ teaspoon freshly ground black pepper

1 Preheat oven to 180°C (350°F).

2 TO PREPARE CHEESE FILLING: Melt butter in a small saucepan. Stir in flour and cook for 30 seconds. Remove from heat and add milk. Stir over medium heat until sauce has boiled and thickened. Cool slightly. Stir through cheeses, eggs, nutmeg and pepper.

3 Cut pastry with a fluted cutter into 10 cm rounds. Place a spoonful of cheese filling on one half of each pastry round. Brush edges with milk and fold pastry in half. Press to seal edges. Glaze pastry tops with egg. Place on a baking tray and bake for 10 to 15 minutes or until puffed and golden.

MAKES 36

CRISPY FRIED CALAMARI

¾ cup (90 g) plain flour

1 teaspoon ground white pepper

4 calamari (squid) tubes

1 egg, lightly beaten

oil for deep frying

lemon wedges, to serve

1 Combine flour and pepper in a bowl. Dip calamari rings in egg and toss in flour.

2 Cook calamari, a few rings at a time, in hot oil until lightly golden. Drain on absorbent paper. Serve with lemon wedges.

SERVES 4

❖ GOAT CHEESE

A relatively hard and dry goat cheese is required for baking. It can be purchased in Greek specialty stores. Goat cheese can be stored in the refrigerator for up to two weeks but it is better to buy it just before using. Once it has been baked or prepared in some other way, it should be eaten very quickly as it will not store well.

BAKED GOAT CHEESE

4 small hard rounds goat cheese
1 tablespoon olive oil
½ teaspoon cracked black pepper
1 tablespoon small oregano leaves

1 Preheat oven to 180°C (350°F).
2 Place cheese rounds on a baking tray. Sprinkle with olive oil. Combine pepper and oregano and sprinkle over cheese.
3 Bake for 10 to 15 minutes or until cheese is golden. Serve with warm crusty bread, marinated vegetables and olives.
SERVES 6 TO 8 AS AN ENTRÉE

OLIVE BREAD

1¼ cups (310 ml) warm milk
2½ teaspoons dry yeast
½ teaspoon sugar
⅓ cup (80 ml) olive oil
1 cup (155 g) black olives, roughly chopped
4 spring onions, finely chopped
3 tablespoons chopped fresh mint
3¾ cups (470 g) plain flour

1 Preheat oven to 200°C (400°F).
2 Place 3 tablespoons milk, yeast and sugar in a large bowl. Leave in a warm place for 5 to 6 minutes or until frothy.
3 Add oil, remaining milk, olives, spring onions, mint and flour. Mix well with a flat knife or with your hand until mixture forms a soft dough. Knead on a lightly floured board for 10 minutes or until dough is smooth and elastic to touch. Place dough in a well oiled bowl and leave covered with a tea-towel for 1 hour, or until dough has doubled in size.
4 Remove dough from bowl and knead lightly. Divide dough in half and shape into loaves (round or square). Stand in a warm place, covered with a tea-towel, for 2 hours or until doubled in size. Place on baking trays and bake for 30 minutes or until cooked. To test, tap top of bread with your fingers or fist. If it is cooked it will sound hollow. Eat bread warm or cold.
MAKES 2 LOAVES

SPICY STUFFED MUSSELS

24 fresh mussels (about 1 kilogram)
⅓ cup (80 ml) oil
2 large onions, very finely chopped
⅓ cup (60 g) long grain rice, well washed
2 tablespoons currants
2 tablespoons pine nuts
¼ teaspoon ground allspice
½ teaspoon ground cinnamon
1 cup (250 ml) water
1 tablespoon fresh lemon juice
lemon wedges, to serve

1 TO CLEAN MUSSELS: Scrub them with a hard brush. Insert the point of a knife and pry them open. Run the knife up and down several times to clean the edges. Remove beards and any shell, sand or grit. Do not separate the mussels. Cover with cold water and leave until ready to use.
2 Heat oil in a frying pan and sauté onions until soft. Add rice, currants, pine nuts, allspice and cinnamon, and stir to combine. Cook over gentle heat for 1 minute. Taste and adjust seasoning then set aside to cool.
3 Drain mussels very well. Place some filling into each mussel and reseal. Layer mussels in a heavy-based pan or flameproof casserole and pour in water and lemon juice. Bring to the boil, reduce heat, cover and simmer for 40 to 50 minutes or until stuffing is tender. Cool to room temperature.
4 Drain mussels and arrange on a serving platter. Cover and chill. Serve with lemon wedges.
SERVES 4

Spicy Stuffed Mussels

Insert the point of a knife and pry mussels open.

Remove beards and any shell, sand or grit.

Place some filling into each mussel and reseal.

STEP-BY-STEP TECHNIQUES

STUFFED VINE LEAVES

250 g vine leaves, fresh or preserved, stalks trimmed

1 tablespoon oil

1 onion, finely chopped

½ cup (90 g) long grain rice

1 cup (250 ml) water

⅓ cup (60 g) pine nuts

½ teaspoon ground cinnamon

freshly ground black pepper

1 tablespoon chopped fresh parsley

1 tomato, peeled, seeded and chopped (optional)

1 lemon, sliced

½ cup (125 ml) oil, extra

Stuffed Vine Leaves

1 Prepare vine leaves. Packaged vine leaves should be rinsed in hot water. Fresh leaves should be washed well, then blanched in boiling salted water for 3 to 4 minutes. Set leaves aside, shiny side down.

2 Heat oil in a pan, and sauté onion until transparent. Add rice and cook until it absorbs the oil. Add water, pine nuts, cinnamon and pepper to taste. Bring to the boil, cover and simmer over gentle heat until rice is cooked. Gently stir through parsley and tomato.

3 Place a teaspoon of filling in the centre of each vine leaf. Fold over top and sides and roll up. Place, seam side down, in a heavy-based pan. Any torn leaves should be used to line the base of the pan and to cover the stuffed vine leaves.

4 Place lemon slices on top of stuffed vine leaves. Pour in extra oil and add sufficient water to cover. Invert a plate over the vine

Prepare vine leaves.

Place filling in centre, fold over top and sides and roll up.

leaves. Cover pan and gently bring to the boil, reduce heat and simmer for 45 minutes.

5 Cool in the pan. Remove plate and drain the stuffed vine leaves. Place on a serving plate, sprinkle with a little extra oil and chill. Serve cold.

MAKES 15 TO 20

CHICKEN AND PINE NUT BALLS

500 g chicken mince

¾ cup (45 g) fresh breadcrumbs

1 egg, lightly beaten

½ cup (60 g) toasted pine nuts

1 tablespoon chopped fresh mint

1 teaspoon freshly ground black pepper

½ cup (60 g) plain flour

oil for shallow frying

CHILLI YOGHURT

¾ cup (180 ml) natural yoghurt

4 red chillies, seeded and chopped

½ teaspoon ground cumin

1 Blend mince, breadcrumbs, egg, pine nuts, mint and pepper in a food processor for 10 to 20 seconds, or until well combined. Roll tablespoons of mixture into balls and toss in flour.

2 Heat oil in a large frypan. Cook chicken balls until golden on all sides. Drain well.

3 TO PREPARE CHILLI YOGHURT: Combine all ingredients and stand for 1 hour. Serve chicken balls with chilli yoghurt as a dipping sauce.

SERVES 4 TO 6

VINE LEAVES WITH FRUIT AND LENTILS

500 g packet vine leaves

½ cup (90 g) lentils, washed

⅓ cup (60 g) burghul, preferably coarse, soaked in warm water for 30 minutes

2 tablespoons oil

1 onion, finely chopped

½ cup (60 g) dried apricots, finely chopped

2 tablespoons currants

1 tablespoon finely chopped fresh mint

1 tablespoon chopped fresh savory

pepper

2 tablespoons fresh lemon juice

1 Rinse vine leaves in hot water and trim stalks. Set aside, shiny side down.

2 Cover lentils with water in a pan, bring to the boil, cover and simmer until tender. Drain and place in a bowl. Drain burghul in a sieve and press out excess water. Place in bowl with lentils.

3 Heat oil and sauté onion until transparent. Drain and add to lentils and burghul. Add fruits, herbs, and pepper to taste. Combine well.

4 Place a spoonful of filling onto each vine leaf, fold over top and sides and roll up. Line a saucepan with damaged leaves. Place stuffed leaves, seam side down, in layers in the pan. Sprinkle with lemon juice. Invert a saucer over leaves and carefully add sufficient water to cover. Bring to the boil, reduce heat and simmer, covered for 45 minutes.

5 Cool to room temperature. Carefully remove to a serving platter, cover and chill until serving time.

MAKES ABOUT 35

❖ VINE LEAVES WITH FRUIT AND LENTILS

This version of stuffed vine leaves comes from the Caucasian region of Armenia. If neither fresh nor dried savory is available, it is preferable to omit it rather than substitute another herb. For a variation, sauté 2 tablespoons of pine nuts in oil and add them to the filling.

Clockwise from rear: Falafel, Eggplant Dip, Filo Spinach Fingers, Tabbouli, Stuffed Vine Leaves

✥ PITA BREAD

This is most familiar to us wrapped around falafel with some hummus and tabbouli, served with chilli or barbecue sauce. It is also very often filled with meat, cut off a rotisserie, or cooked as kebabs. Pita bread is ideal for serving with dips at a party instead of crackers. It can also be slit open and filled with a variety of salads and meats for superb sandwiches, or simply rolled around various fillings. A good way to use stale pita bread is to brush it with butter or oil, sprinkle with poppy seeds or sesame seeds, or with crushed garlic, and heat in the oven. Serve as an appetiser on its own or with soup.

Breads

Traditional breads eaten in Greece and Middle Eastern countries include the flat breads, of which pita and pide are the most common. Flat breads are served with every meal and often form a meal in themselves when filled or served with dips and salads.

PITA BREAD

4 cups (500 g) plain flour
¾ teaspoon salt
20 g compressed yeast
1¼ cups (310 ml) lukewarm water
2 tablespoons olive oil
extra plain flour

1 Sift flour and salt into a large bowl. Crumble yeast into a small bowl and stir in ¼ cup (60 ml) warm water. Sprinkle yeast with a little flour, cover with a cloth and place in a warm position until mixture becomes frothy.

2 Make a well in the centre of the flour and pour in yeast mixture, oil, and sufficient water to make a soft dough. Place dough on a lightly floured surface and knead until it is very elastic. Place in a lightly oiled bowl, cover with a cloth and set in a warm position for 45 minutes, until it doubles in bulk. Punch down and divide into 4 equal portions. Knead each piece into a ball, cover with a towel and leave for 20 minutes.

3 Preheat oven to 250°C (500°F).

4 Sprinkle 2 large baking trays with flour. Roll balls of dough into very thin circles and place on trays. Cover with a cloth and leave to rest for a further 20 minutes.

5 Bake for 10 minutes, or until bread puffs up in the centre and is a delicate brown. Remove bread from trays and wrap up in foil for 10 minutes. When bread is unwrapped the tops will have fallen and there will be a shallow pocket of air in the bread.

MAKES 4

TURKISH FLAT BREAD
Pide

⅓ cup (80 ml) warm water
pinch sugar
3 teaspoons yeast
2½ cups (310 g) plain flour
½ teaspoon salt
2 tablespoons olive oil
¾ cup (180 ml) warm water, extra
1 egg, lightly beaten
dill seeds, fennel seeds or sesame seeds

1 Preheat oven to 220°C (425°F).

2 Place water, sugar and yeast in a large bowl. Leave in a warm place for 5 minutes or until frothy.

3 Add flour, salt, oil and extra water. Mix to a soft and sticky dough. Knead for 10 minutes on a lightly floured board. The stickiness of the dough will decrease as you knead.

4 Place dough in a well oiled bowl. Cover with plastic wrap and leave until doubled in size. Place large baking trays in oven and heat them for at least 20 minutes.

5 Divide dough in half. Make each into a ball. With the palm of your hand push down on balls. Push and stretch them until they are 20 cm x 30 cm oval shape. Brush with egg and sprinkle with seeds. Slide dough into oven onto baking trays. Bake for 6 to 8 minutes or until golden and puffed. Pide is best eaten straight from the oven.

MAKES 2 LARGE BREADS

EGGPLANT, TOMATO AND OLIVE PIDE

1 quantity pide dough (recipe page 24)

FILLING

2 large eggplants (aubergine), cut into 2 cm thick slices

salt

4 tablespoons olive oil

2 onions, chopped

3 tomatoes, peeled and chopped

¾ cup (125 g) black olives, pitted

½ bunch fresh basil, chopped

beaten egg or milk, for brushing

dill seeds

1 Preheat oven to 220°C (425°F).

2 Prepare pide dough. Allow to double in size. Knead lightly and divide into 6 equal portions. Roll each portion into a ball, cover with a tea-towel and leave for 30 minutes.

3 TO PREPARE FILLING: Sprinkle eggplant with salt and leave for 20 to 30 minutes. Wash and dry. Using about 3 tablespoons oil, brush eggplant with oil and grill on both sides until golden. Heat 1 tablespoon oil in a pan. Sauté onions for 2 minutes. Add tomatoes and simmer for 4 minutes. Add olives, basil and eggplant.

4 Heat baking trays in oven for at least 20 minutes.

5 TO ASSEMBLE PIDE: Roll each ball into a 12 cm x 22 cm oval. Divide filling among them, leaving a 2 cm border. Bring the long edges into the centre and press between fingers to seal along centre seam. Seal ends well. Brush with beaten egg or milk and sprinkle with dill seeds. Bake on hot oven trays for 6 to 8 minutes. Serve immediately.

SERVES 6

CAPSICUM AND FETA PIDE

1 quantity pide dough (recipe page 24)

FILLING

1 tablespoon olive oil

2 cloves garlic, crushed

1 red capsicum (pepper), seeded and chopped

1 green capsicum (pepper), seeded and chopped

375 g feta cheese, crumbled

2 tablespoons fresh oregano

2 eggs, lightly beaten

1 teaspoon freshly ground black pepper

beaten egg or milk, for brushing

dill seeds

1 Preheat oven to 220°C (425°F).

2 Prepare pide dough. Allow to double in size. Knead lightly and divide into 6 equal portions. Roll each portion into a ball, cover with a tea-towel and leave for 30 minutes.

3 TO PREPARE FILLING: Heat oil in a frying pan and sauté garlic, red and green capsicum for 4 to 5 minutes or until soft. Set aside to cool, then combine with feta, oregano, egg and pepper in a bowl.

4 Heat baking trays in oven for at least 20 minutes.

5 TO ASSEMBLE PIDE: Roll each ball into a 12 cm x 22 cm oval. Divide filling among them, leaving a 2 cm border. Bring the long edges into the centre and press between fingers to seal along centre seam. Seal ends well. Brush with beaten egg or milk and sprinkle with dill seeds. Bake on hot oven trays for 6 to 8 minutes. Serve immediately.

SERVES 6

✥ PIDE

This is the traditional Turkish flat bread, similar to pita, the flat bread eaten in Greece and Lebanon.

Filled pide is often called Turkish pizza and in Turkish pide shops, the variety of fillings is huge. Instead of capsicum in the Capsicum and Feta Pide, try substituting fresh herbs such as mint, parsley or dill. Spinach mixed with feta and egg is another popular combination; or minced lamb with chillies, tomatoes, herbs and garlic. For some more ideas, visit a Turkish takeaway shop.

Seafood

Fish is a favourite in the Middle East, particularly in the western area. Fish is also very popular in Greece. Stewing is a common cooking method, as is grilling over wood or charcoal. When purchasing fish, look for signs of freshness: bright, clear eyes, red gills, fresh sea aroma and scales that are not too easy to remove.

Octopus and squid appear in many dishes and are often marinated or barbecued.

It is recommended that fish be purchased and cooked on the same day. If you are lucky enough to have an excellent fish market nearby, this is the place to purchase your good quality, fresh fish. Fish must never be overcooked.

In this chapter are many easy, delicious recipes for seafood dishes including fish soup, fish in filo pastry, pilavs, dishes with prawns or mussels and many more.

Spicy Algerian Sardines and Tomato Roasted Octopus

PREPARATION OF FISH

To prepare a whole fish for cooking, wipe it over with a damp cloth and check for scales near the head and fins. If further scaling is necessary, use a teaspoon and scrape lightly but firmly from the tail to the head on both sides. This is best done under running water because the scales then collect in the sink and can be easily discarded. If desired, the fins may be trimmed and the tail neatened with a pair of scissors. The eyes may be removed but are better left in because when they turn white you know the fish is cooked. If you find them unsightly cover them with a garnish before serving. You can also tell when the fish is cooked by testing the flesh: if it flakes the fish is ready.

Open the cavity of the fish and sprinkle into it about 2 teaspoons of salt. Take a wad of absorbent paper and clean well down the backbone to remove any blood spots. Rinse with cold water. Pat the fish dry, cover and refrigerate until used.

Fish cutlets need only to be wiped over with a clean damp cloth. Fillets should have all the bones removed. If you have trouble removing the small, fine bones, use a pair of clean, sterilised tweezers. Although tedious, this is worthwhile if preparing fillets for children or fussy eaters. Use a sharp knife when skinning fillets. Make a small cut near the tail end of the fillet, taking care not to cut all the way through. Dip the fingers of your other hand in salt so your fingers won't slip, and grasp the tail end below the cut. Place the knife in the cut and work towards the head end using a side-to-side cutting action. Hold the knife at a 45 degree angle, making sure not to cut the skin.

Scaling can be done with a teaspoon, lightly running from tail to head on both sides.

The tails and fins may be trimmed and neatened with a pair of sharp kitchen scissors.

Sprinkle salt inside the cavity and, with a wad of absorbent paper, remove any blood spots.

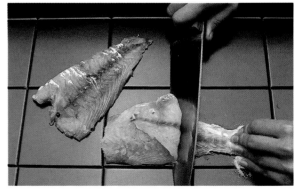

When skinning fillets, work from tail to head, holding the knife at a 45 degree angle.

Fish Soup with Egg and Lemon

500 g fish fillets

4 cups (1 litre) fish stock

3 egg yolks

juice 1 large lemon

1 Prepare the fillets as directed on page 28. Bring stock to the boil. Carefully slip fillets into the stock and simmer for 5 to 7 minutes or until cooked when tested. Remove fillets from stock and cut into 2 cm strips; keep warm.

2 Beat egg yolks and lemon juice lightly in a small bowl. Gradually add ½ cup (125 ml) of hot stock, whisking constantly. Return to pan and cook over very gentle heat until soup thickens slightly. Add fish and serve hot.

SERVES 4

Calamari in Red Wine

8 calamari (squid), cut in half

1 tablespoon olive oil

2 cups (500 ml) red wine

6 black peppercorns

6 coriander seeds

2 cups (500 ml) fish stock

1 Place all ingredients in a large saucepan. Simmer gently for 1 hour or until tender. Water may be added during cooking to ensure pan does not simmer dry.

2 Serve calamari hot with okra and tomatoes or cold in a salad.

SERVES 4

Spicy Algerian Sardines

1 kg fresh sardines

2 tablespoons ground cumin

2 teaspoons chilli powder

3 cloves garlic, crushed

2 teaspoons freshly ground black pepper

1½ cups (185 g) plain flour

2 eggs, lightly beaten

oil for shallow frying

1 Make a slit on the underside of sardines, gut and remove backbone.

2 Combine cumin, chilli, garlic, pepper and flour in a bowl. Dip sardines into egg and then roll in spicy flour. Repeat with egg and flour, until all the sardines have been coated.

3 Heat oil in a large frying pan. Cook sardines 1 to 2 minutes each side or until brown and tender. Serve as a starter or with salad as a main meal.

SERVES 6 TO 8

Tomato Roasted Octopus

1 kg octopus, cleaned

MARINADE

2 tablespoons olive oil

2 cloves garlic, crushed

2 tablespoons red wine vinegar

½ cup (125 ml) tomato purée

1 teaspoon sugar

1 tablespoon chopped fresh oregano

1 Combine all ingredients in a bowl. Add octopus, cover and refrigerate overnight or for 3 to 4 hours, minimum.

2 Roast octopus under a hot grill for 2 to 3 minutes each side. Serve hot or cold.

SERVES 4

✛ OCTOPUS

You don't have to remove the skin of octopus as it does not affect the flavour. However, the gut must be removed by slitting open the head. Because it is quite tough, octopus should be tenderised before cooking, unless the recipe involves long periods of cooking such as in Red Wine Baby Octopus.

✥ FRIED MUSSELS

This dish is popular in the Middle East with variations according to the region. The Turkish version is dipped in beer instead of egg.

It makes an excellent entrée, much of which can be prepared in advance.

MUSSELS TARATOR

1 kg mussels in shells

½ cup (60 g) seasoned plain flour

2 eggs, beaten

oil for deep frying

TARATOR SAUCE

200 g pine nuts, hazelnuts or walnuts

2 slices white bread, crusts removed

2 to 4 cloves garlic, crushed

juice of 2 lemons or 4 tablespoons vinegar

1 cup (250 ml) olive oil or fish stock

1 Scrub mussels and pry open with a knife. Trim beards and carefully remove mussels from shells. Wash and pat dry.

2 Dip mussels in flour, shaking to remove excess. Coat with egg and drain.

3 Heat oil and fry mussels in batches until golden, about 3 minutes. Drain on crumpled absorbent paper.

4 TO PREPARE TARATOR SAUCE: Finely grind nuts in a mortar and pestle or food processor. Soak bread in water and squeeze dry. Blend nuts and bread. Add garlic, lemon juice, and olive oil and continue pounding or processing until ingredients are combined. Serve mussels hot, with Tarator Sauce.

SERVES 4

RED WINE BABY OCTOPUS

1 kg baby octopus, cleaned

4 cups (1 litre) red wine

3 cloves garlic, crushed

2 onions, sliced

2 tablespoons fresh lemon juice

1 teaspoon ground oregano

1 teaspoon chilli powder

Red Wine Baby Octopus

1 Place all ingredients in a large saucepan. Simmer for 1 to 1½ hours or until octopus is tender.

SERVES 4 TO 6

CORIANDER PRAWNS

1 tablespoon oil

4 cloves garlic, crushed

2 small red chillies, seeded and chopped

1 teaspoon paprika

1 teaspoon cumin seeds

750 g green (uncooked) king prawns (shrimps), peeled and deveined

½ bunch fresh coriander, chopped

1 Heat oil in a large frying pan. Cook garlic, chillies, paprika and cumin seeds for 2 minutes.

2 Add prawns to pan and toss in spiced oil. Cook for 4 to 5 minutes or until pink. Stir through coriander. Serve with rice or noodles.

SERVES 4

REDFISH FILO PARCELS

12 sheets filo pastry

60 g butter, melted or 3 tablespoons olive oil

FILLING

4 x 200 g redfish fillets (or sea bream or mullet)

1 cup (250 ml) water

1 bay leaf

4 black peppercorns

30 g butter

⅓ cup (40 g) plain flour

1 tablespoon fresh lemon juice

3 tablespoons white wine

2 teaspoons chopped fresh dill

1 TO PREPARE FILLING: Place fish, water, bay leaf and peppercorns in a large frying pan. Simmer fish 2 to 3 minutes each side or until cooked. Remove fish from pan, drain liquid and set aside.

2 Melt butter in a small frying pan. Add flour and cook for 1 minute. Remove from heat and add reserved liquid, lemon juice and wine, mixing until smooth. Return to heat and stir until sauce boils and thickens. Flake fish with fork and fold through sauce with dill.

3 Preheat oven to 180°C (350°F).

4 TO ASSEMBLE PARCELS: Brush one sheet of pastry lightly with butter. Fold into thirds lengthways so you have one long strip of pastry. Place one spoonful of filling at one end of the pastry. Pick up one corner of the pastry and fold it over the filling diagonally. Take opposite corner and fold it diagonally. Keep folding alternate corners until reaching the end of the pastry, ending up with a triangle. Brush with butter and place on a baking tray. Repeat with remaining pastry and filling.

5 Bake for 15 minutes or until pastry is golden. Serve as a starter or with salad as a main meal.

MAKES 12

Redfish Filo Parcels

❖ FILO PASTRY

Brushing with butter gives a delicious but rich flavour. Brushing with olive oil gives a much lighter flavour and is the low cholesterol alternative.

HERB AND PEPPER BREAM

2 x 500 g sea bream, cleaned

HERB AND PEPPER MARINADE
⅓ cup (80 ml) olive oil
⅓ cup (80 ml) white wine
2 teaspoons cracked black pepper
1 tablespoon chopped fresh dill
1 tablespoon lemon thyme

1 Preheat oven to 180°C (350°F).
2 TO PREPARE MARINADE: Combine all ingredients in a bowl and mix well.
3 Place bream on separate pieces of foil. Brush both sides of fish with marinade. Seal foil well, bake for 20 to 25 minutes or until fish flakes. Alternatively, cook over hot coals.

SERVES 2 TO 4

MUSSEL AND PRAWN PILAV

24 green (uncooked) mussels
1 cup (250 ml) water
1 tablespoon olive oil
6 spring onions, chopped
4 cups (1 litre) water, extra
2 cups (440 g) rice, washed and drained
24 cooked prawns (shrimps), shelled and deveined
2 teaspoons grated lemon rind
2 teaspoons chopped fresh oregano
1 teaspoon freshly ground black pepper

1 Wash and scrub mussels until clean. Place mussels with water in a saucepan and simmer for 4 to 5 minutes or until shells open. Discard any unopened shells.
2 Remove mussels from shells and set aside. Strain cooking liquid and set aside.

3 Heat oil in a large pan. Add spring onions and cook for 1 minute. Add extra water and mussel cooking liquid. Heat until simmering. Add rice and cook slowly for 15 to 20 minutes or until liquid is absorbed.
4 Return mussels to pan with prawns, lemon rind, oregano and pepper. Stir for 2 minutes or until heated through.

SERVES 4 TO 6

FISH WITH TOMATOES

4 small fish or 500 g fish fillets (sea bream or snapper)

SAUCE
¾ cup (180 ml) olive oil
4 onions, thinly sliced
1 carrot, diced
3 large cloves garlic, chopped
500 g tomatoes, peeled, seeded and chopped
2 teaspoons tomato paste
1 teaspoon paprika
½ cup (125 ml) water
1 cup (250 ml) fish stock

1 Clean fish or fillets as described on page 28.
3 TO PREPARE SAUCE: Heat half the oil in a pan. Sauté onions and carrot for 15 minutes over medium heat, stirring constantly. Add garlic and cook a further 3 minutes. Add tomatoes, tomato paste, paprika, water and stock. Bring to the boil, reduce heat and simmer for 20 minutes.
2 Place fish in sauce, cover and cook over gentle heat, 20 to 25 minutes for whole fish or 10 to 15 minutes for fillets, until cooked (fish flakes with a fork). Remove from heat and leave to cool in pan. Chill before serving.

SERVES 4

✣ FISH WITH TOMATOES

This dish should be served chilled. If serving as a main course, small, whole fish are best but fillets may be substituted.

Herb and Pepper Bream

**◆ POACHED
WHOLE FISH
WITH RICE**

*Popular along the
Mediterranean coast, this
recipe has few ingredients
but shows resourceful use
of the fish stock produced.
It is used to cook the rice
and is also turned into
a sauce to accompany
the dish.*

POACHED WHOLE FISH WITH RICE

1½ kg whole fish

⅓ cup (80 ml) olive oil

3 onions, thinly sliced

6 cups (1½ litres) water

½ teaspoon ground cumin

1½ cups (300 g) rice, washed

juice 2 to 3 lemons

1 Prepare the fish as directed on page 28. Cover and refrigerate.

2 Heat oil and sauté onions over moderately low heat until soft and just starting to turn golden. Add water, bring to the boil, reduce heat and simmer until onions are very soft.

3 Remove onions, reserving liquid, and push onions through a sieve. Return onions to liquid and add cumin. Bring to the boil. Slide fish into boiling liquid, reduce heat and poach for 20 minutes or until cooked when tested. Carefully remove fish and place on a board to skin and fillet. Cover and keep warm.

4 Measure out 4 cups (1 litre) of liquid (reserving the rest as sauce for serving) and bring to the boil. Add rice, return to the boil. Cover and simmer until rice is tender and liquid absorbed, about 20 minutes. While rice is cooking, flavour remaining

stock with lemon juice. Bring to the boil then simmer uncovered until flavour develops and mixture reduces slightly.

5 To serve, fluff up rice and arrange on a serving platter. Place fish on top and moisten with half of sauce. Serve with remaining sauce and flat bread. If desired, garnish fish platter with spring onion curls, lemon slices, quartered cherry tomatoes, and a sprinkling of paprika or chilli powder.

SERVES 4 TO 6

BARBECUED TROUT

4 x 450 g trout

1 teaspoon paprika

80 g butter, melted

lemon wedges

few sprigs fresh tarragon or fresh dill

1 Prepare fish as directed on page 28 and season with paprika. Lightly brush long skewers with melted butter and skewer fish lengthways. Alternatively, use a hinged barbecue grid or a special fish grid.

2 Cook fish over glowing coals, turning and brushing with melted butter, until cooked. Serve hot with lemon wedges and garnish with tarragon or dill.

SERVES 4

*Poached Whole
Fish with Rice*

Push the sautéed and simmered onions through a sieve.

Skin and fillet the poached fish, keeping it warm until required.

Slowly sprinkle the rice into boiling water and simmer for about 20 minutes.

Barbecued Trout

STEP-BY-STEP TECHNIQUES

BAKED FISH WITH CRACKED WHEAT

¾ cup (135 g) cracked wheat (burghul)

1½ cups (1½ litres) hot water

1 onion, roughly chopped

250 g fish fillets, skinned and cut into small pieces

½ teaspoon grated orange rind

2 teaspoons very finely chopped fresh coriander

salt and pepper

2 tablespoons oil

2 onions, sliced (extra)

pinch saffron threads

1 Soak burghul in the hot water for 30 minutes; drain and press out liquid.

2 Blend onion in a food processor for 30 seconds. Add fish and process until mixture is very smooth. Chill for 10 minutes.

3 Preheat oven to 200°C (400°F).

4 Place burghul, fish mixture, orange rind and coriander in a bowl. Season with salt and pepper to taste. Mix thoroughly, then knead in a bowl for 5 minutes or until smooth.

5 Heat 1 tablespoon of oil and sauté the extra onions until golden. Cover saffron with a little boiling water, cool then squeeze threads to extract colour. Add saffron and liquid to onions and season to taste.

6 Spread half the fish mixture in a small, lightly greased, round ovenproof dish. Top with onion mixture. Cover with remaining fish mixture and smooth the top. Score into diamond shapes and sprinkle with 1 tablespoon oil. Bake for 25 to 30 minutes. Cool, then cut into serving pieces.

SERVES 4

Add fish to processed onion and process until smooth.

Mix burghul, fish, orange rind and coriander in a bowl, with salt and pepper to taste.

Spread half the mixture in an ovenproof dish and top with onions.

Baked Fish with Cracked Wheat

⬩✛⬩ **CRACKED WHEAT**

This is made from whole wheat grains which are cracked open. Burghul is made from hulled wheat grains (not whole). However, they can be used in the same way in all recipes. Both need soaking before use.

SPICY BAKED FISH

¾ cup (90 g) finely chopped almonds

5 cloves garlic, chopped

⅓ cup (80 ml) fresh lemon juice

⅓ cup chopped fresh coriander

4 small red chillies, seeded and chopped

1 tablespoon oil

2 teaspoons cracked black pepper

1 to 1½ kg bream, cleaned and patted dry

1 Preheat oven to 180°C (350°F).

2 Mix together almonds, garlic, lemon juice, coriander, chillies, oil and pepper.

3 Place fish in a large baking dish. Spoon mixture over fish and inside cavity.

4 Bake fish covered for 30 minutes or until fish flakes. Serve with sauce from dish and steamed basmati rice.

SERVES 6

MACKEREL WITH NUTS AND HERBS

4 x 350 g mackerel, cleaned and patted dry

STUFFING

1 tablespoon olive oil

2 onions, finely chopped

⅓ cup (40 g) ground walnuts

⅓ cup (40 g) ground hazelnuts

½ cup (90 g) raisins

½ teaspoon ground cinnamon

3 tablespoons chopped fresh parsley

2 tablespoons chopped fresh dill

1 teaspoon freshly ground black pepper

2 eggs, lightly beaten

2 cups (250 g) dry breadcrumbs

oil for shallow frying

lemon wedges, to serve

1 TO PREPARE STUFFING: Heat oil in a frying pan. Sauté onions for 2 minutes or until soft. Add walnuts and hazelnuts. Cook 2 minutes. Add raisins, cinnamon, parsley, dill and pepper. Stir and cook for 1 minute.

2 Stuff the fish cavities with prepared stuffing and secure with toothpicks. Dip each fish in egg and roll in breadcrumbs. Shallow fry in hot oil for 3 to 4 minutes each side or until crisp and tender. Serve with lemon.

SERVES 4

FISH PATTIES

750 g fish fillets

2 slices stale bread, crusts removed

1 onion, finely chopped

1 egg, beaten

2 tablespoons finely chopped fresh parsley

½ teaspoon salt

freshly ground black pepper

½ teaspoon cumin

pinch of saffron soaked in 1 teaspoon warm water

cornflour

oil for deep frying

1 Remove skin and bones from fish and blend to a paste in an electric blender. You may have to do this in 2 to 3 batches.

2 Place fish in a mixing bowl and add all remaining ingredients except cornflour and oil. Mix until thoroughly combined.

3 Shape mixture into small balls and roll in cornflour. Heat oil for deep frying and fry balls for 4 to 5 minutes until golden brown. Drain on absorbent papper and serve immediately.

SERVES 6

BAKED FISH WITH ZUCCHINI AND TOMATOES

1½ kg whole fish

salt and freshly ground black pepper

2 tablespoons olive oil

2 onions, sliced

2 cloves garlic, crushed

2 tablespoons chopped fresh parsley

**2 tablespoons chopped fresh mint or
½ teaspoon dried mint**

3 tomatoes, peeled, seeded and chopped

½ teaspoon sugar

pinch cinnamon

¾ cup (180 ml) water

**6 small zucchini (courgettes), cut into 2½ cm
pieces**

juice ½ lemon

1 Preheat oven to 180°C (350°F).

2 Wash and dry fish and sprinkle inside and out with ½ teaspoon salt and pepper.

3 Heat oil in a large frying pan and sauté onions until light golden and soft. Add garlic, parsley, mint, tomatoes, salt and pepper to taste, sugar and cinnamon. Cook for 1 minute. Add water, cover and simmer for 3 minutes.

4 Add zucchini and fish. Cover and bake for 20 to 25 minutes, until fish is tender. Sprinkle with lemon juice to serve.

SERVES 6

FISH WITH GARLIC AND NUT SAUCE

2 kg whole fish

salt and freshly ground black pepper

fresh lemon juice

olive oil

1 lettuce

lemon wedges, to garnish

GARLIC AND NUT SAUCE

1 cup (200 g) pine nuts, hazelnuts or walnuts

2 slices white bread, crusts removed

2 to 4 cloves garlic, crushed

juice 2 lemons or 4 tablespoons vinegar

**1 cup (250 ml) olive oil or fish stock
or a combination of both**

1 Preheat oven to 180°C (350°F).

2 Clean fish as directed on page 28 and slash in the thickest section. Season with salt, pepper and lemon juice and rub with a little olive oil.

3 Pour some oil into a baking dish. Place fish in and cover with foil. Bake, basting occasionally for 30 to 40 minutes or until fish is cooked.

4 Wash and dry lettuce and arrange on a serving plate. Carefully place fish on top garnishing it with lemon wedges. Serve with olives, sliced radish, pickles, toasted and untoasted pine nuts, chopped spring onions and parsley, and Garlic and Nut Sauce.

5 TO PREPARE GARLIC SAUCE: Finely grind nuts in a mortar and pestle or food processor. Soak bread in water and squeeze dry. Blend nuts and bread. Add garlic, lemon juice and olive oil. Continue pounding or processing until ingredients are combined.

SERVES 6

✛ GARLIC AND NUT SAUCE

This sauce, also called Tarator Sauce, is made with pine nuts, hazelnuts or walnuts, depending upon the region from which the recipe comes. For fish dishes, fish stock can replace all or part of the olive oil.

If using pine nuts, flavour the sauce with lemon juice; use vinegar if using hazelnuts or walnuts. Peeled, unroasted hazelnuts will give a lighter coloured sauce than shelled hazelnuts. Roasted hazelnuts will change the flavour of the sauce.

If using very fresh breadcrumbs, you don't need to soak them first.

Poultry

Chicken and game such as quail are popular in Greece and the
Middle East, and, like fish, often cooked over coals. Small birds are often
marinated for a few hours in a mixture of olive oil and lemon juice, with
salt and pepper to taste, drained, then cooked over glowing coals.
In Turkey, it is common to flavour poultry with a little cinnamon,
and a pinch can be added to the marinade.

Poultry is stuffed, roasted, stewed and often served with rice in pilavs.
Nuts, herbs and spices are used as flavourings, in stuffings and in sauces to
make delicious dishes.

Chicken and Vegetable Casserole

CHICKEN AND RAISIN PASTRIES

1 whole chicken breast

60 g butter

3 tablespoons plain flour

1½ cups (375 ml) milk

½ teaspoon freshly ground black pepper

½ teaspoon ground cinnamon

⅓ cup (60 g) raisins

5 sheets filo pastry

½ cup (125 ml) oil

1 Steam chicken breast over boiling water for 10 to 15 minutes or until cooked. Alternatively, poach in a little water. When cool, remove skin and bones and finely chop flesh.

2 Melt butter in a pan, add flour and cook over moderate heat for a few minutes, stirring. Gradually add milk, bring to the boil. Season to taste with pepper and add cinnamon and raisins. Simmer for 2 minutes. Set aside to cool, covering surface with a piece of plastic wrap to prevent a skin forming. When sauce is cool, stir through chicken.

3 Preheat oven to 180°C (350°F).

4 Cut pastry lengthways into three strips. Cover with a tea-towel. Take one strip of pastry, brush lightly with oil and place a little filling at one end. Fold over end and sides and roll up neatly. Place seam side down on a greased baking tray. Repeat with remaining pastry and filling. Brush tops with a little oil and bake for 20 to 25 minutes or until golden. Serve warm.

MAKES 15

✛ PREPARING WHOLE CHICKENS

Before cooking, whole chickens should be cleaned. Remove the fat from the cavity and check the skin for fine feathers. These are best removed using a pair of clean, sterilised tweezers. Clean the backbone of the chicken well, wash the bird inside and out, dry it and keep it refrigerated until ready to use.

CHICKEN AND VEGETABLE CASSEROLE

500 g eggplant (aubergine)

salt

4 tablespoons olive oil

6 chicken breast fillets

2 cloves garlic, crushed

400 g okra, sliced

3 zucchini (courgettes), sliced

4 tomatoes, peeled and roughly chopped

1 cup (150 g) black olives

1 Roughly chop eggplant and sprinkle with salt. Leave for 20 to 30 minutes, then wash and drain well.

2 Heat 2 tablespoons oil in pan and cook chicken for 2 to 3 minutes each side or until golden and tender. Set aside.

3 Heat remaining oil in pan and sauté garlic for 1 minute. Add okra, zucchini and tomatoes. Sauté for a further 3 to 4 minutes or until vegetables are soft. Stir through olives and chicken. Heat 1 minute and serve.

SERVES 6

HOT POT CHICKEN

2 tablespoons oil

1½ kg chicken, cut into serving pieces

2 cloves garlic, crushed

½ cup (125 ml) dry sherry

440 g canned tomatoes

2 tablespoons tomato paste (concentrated tomato purée)

½ cup (125 ml) chicken stock

60 g Parmesan cheese, grated

1 Heat oil in a large frying pan. Add chicken pieces and cook until brown.

2 Add garlic, sherry, tomatoes, tomato paste and stock. Cover and simmer for 35 to 40 minutes or until chicken is tender. Sprinkle with Parmesan cheese and serve with noodles.

SERVES 4

CHICKEN LIVER PILAV WITH NUTS

500 g chicken livers

1 cup (200 g) rice

75 g butter

salt and freshly ground black pepper

1 bunch spring onions, thinly sliced

⅓ cup (45 g) pine nuts

¼ cup (30 g) almonds, slivered

2 tablespoons seeded raisins

2 tomatoes, peeled, seeded and chopped

2 cups (500 ml) water

extra spring onions, to garnish

1 Rinse chicken livers, trim as necessary, cutting off any dark sections and dry them. Cover rice with boiling water, stir well and pour into a sieve. Rinse with cold water until water runs clear.

2 Heat 45 g butter in a pan, and cook livers for 3 minutes until brown but still pink inside. Season with salt and pepper and remove from pan. Add half the spring onions to the pan and sauté until lightly golden. Drain and set aside.

3 Heat remaining butter in a heavy-based pan. Sauté remaining spring onions for a few minutes, then add pine nuts, almonds and raisins and sauté for 2 minutes. Add tomatoes, rice and water with salt and pepper to taste.

4 Bring to the boil, reduce heat, cover and simmer for 20 minutes. Top the rice with extra spring onions and livers. Reduce heat to very low and cook for a further 10 to 15 minutes. Fluff up rice with a fork and serve hot.

SERVES 4

POACHED CHICKEN WITH FRUIT

6 chicken breasts, halved

1 teaspoon freshly ground black pepper

60 g ghee

1 teaspoon ground cinnamon

1¼ cups (310 ml) water

1 cup (125 g) dried apricots

¾ cup (150 g) prunes, pitted

¾ cup (125 g) sultanas

1 Wipe chicken breasts and season lightly with pepper. Heat ghee in a frying pan and sauté chicken until browned on both sides. Combine cinnamon and water and add to pan. Bring to the boil, reduce heat, cover and simmer for 10 minutes.

2 Add dried fruits to chicken and continue simmering for a further 5 minutes, or until chicken is tender. Add more water if necessary. Serve hot with rice.

SERVES 6

✣ **PILAV**

Pilavs originated in Persia, (called pulau), and were then introduced to Middle Eastern countries.

A pilav or pilaf is a dish based on rice and using one or more other ingredients, either poultry, meat or vegetables. Often added to pilafs are butter, nuts, shellfish, fried fruits and various spices. Saffron is a very common ingredient too.

Pilavs are usually made with long grain rice, although the Turkish seem to prefer short grain rice. Other grains such as cracked wheat (burghul) can also be used.

Orange and Chicken Pilav

750 g chicken breast fillets
500 g carrots, peeled and diced
100 g butter
¼ cup (45 g) candied orange peel
½ cup (90 g) blanched almonds, split
3 cups (550 g) rice, cooked
pinch saffron threads, soaked

1 Place chicken in a pan with water to cover. Bring to the boil, reduce heat, cover and simmer for 10 minutes. Allow to cool in juice. Remove and slice breasts.

2 Cook carrots in 1 cup (250 ml) water until tender and water has evaporated. Add 75 g butter to pan and sauté carrots over moderate heat for 5 minutes. Add candied orange peel, reduce heat and cook for 10 minutes, stirring.

3 Melt remaining butter and sauté almonds over gentle heat until golden. Set aside.

4 Place half the rice in a pan. Cover with half the carrots, chicken and almonds. Cover with a little more rice and remaining carrots, chicken and almonds. Top with remaining rice. Cover and cook over very gentle heat for 30 minutes if necessary.

5 Just before serving, pour saffron and liquid over rice. Cover and leave for a few minutes. Stir saffron through rice, serve hot.

SERVES 6

Golden Roast Chicken

1½ kg chicken
1 onion, chopped
1 teaspoon salt
2½ cups (625 ml) natural yoghurt
2 cups (500 g) cooked rice
250 g cooked or shelled peas
½ cup (60 g) pine nuts
salt and pepper

1 Preheat oven to 180°C (350°F).

2 Place chicken in a non-metallic dish.

3 Combine onion, salt and yoghurt, spoon over chicken and marinate in refrigerator for several hours. Remove excess marinade.

4 Combine remaining ingredients and season to taste. Stuff chicken with mixture. Truss and bake for 1¼ hours or until tender.

SERVES 8

Circassian Chicken

1½ kg chicken
1 large onion, chopped
1 bay leaf
8 celery leaves
6 black peppercorns
¾ cup (100 g) ground walnuts, almonds or hazelnuts
½ cup (60 g) dry breadcrumbs
1 teaspoon paprika
1 tablespoon oil

1 Place chicken in a large saucepan. Add onion, bay leaf, celery leaves, peppercorns and water to cover. Bring to the boil, reduce heat, cover and simmer until tender. Skim occasionally. Remove chicken from saucepan and set aside to cool.

2 Strain cooking liquid and place 2 cups (500 ml) in a clean pan. Add nuts and breadcrumbs and stir to combine. Bring to the boil, reduce heat and simmer, stirring, until sauce thickens.

3 Either joint chicken or take meat off bones and slice neatly. Arrange on a serving plate and pour over most of the sauce.

4 Combine paprika and oil stirring well; drizzle this over chicken. Serve with rice and remaining sauce. Alternatively, arrange chicken over a mound of cooked rice and pour over sauce; garnish with paprika and oil. May be served warm or cold.

SERVES 4

  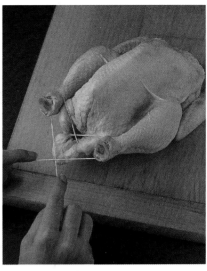

Combine onion, salt and yoghurt, spoon over chicken and marinate several hours. Wipe excess marinade from chicken.

Combine remaining ingredients and season to taste. Stuff chicken with mixture.

Truss chicken using string, then bake for 1¼ hours or until tender.

Golden Roast Chicken

GRILLED QUAIL WITH GARLIC SAUCE

6 quail

MARINADE

3 tablespoons olive oil

juice 2 lemons

2 cloves garlic, crushed

salt and freshly ground black pepper

GARLIC SAUCE

4 large cloves garlic, chopped

½ teaspoon salt

¾ cup to 1 cup (180 to 250 ml) olive oil

juice 1 to 2 lemons

white pepper

Grilled Quail with Garlic Sauce

1 TO PREPARE MARINADE: Combine oil, lemon juice and garlic and season with salt and pepper to taste. Pour over quail. Marinate for 2 hours.

2 Drain quail. Cook over glowing coals or under a preheated grill for 20 minutes, turning occasionally and brushing with reserved marinade.

3 TO PREPARE GARLIC SAUCE: Using a mortar and pestle, crush and stir garlic and salt until a smooth paste forms and salt dissolves.

4 Gradually add oil, stirring well between additions. When 1 to 2 tablespoons of oil have been blended in, add a few drops of lemon juice. Continue carefully with remaining oil and lemon juice but stop adding oil when mixture looks as if it could separate. Stir through white pepper to taste and chill until serving.

Alternatively, the sauce can be prepared in a food processor. First blend garlic and salt. Then with the motor running, gradually add oil through the feeder tube, alternating with lemon juice as above. Stir through white pepper and chill.

5 Serve quail with Garlic Sauce separately.

SERVES 6

CURRY ROASTED CHICKEN

1.6 kg chicken, cleaned and dried

4 thick slices lemon rind

40 g butter, softened

2 teaspoons curry powder

½ teaspoon ground cinnamon

½ teaspoon chilli powder

1 teaspoon ground black pepper

1 Preheat oven to 180°C (350°F).

2 Place lemon rind inside chicken cavity.

3 Combine butter, curry powder, cinnamon, chilli powder and black pepper in a small bowl. Rub spice mixture all over chicken.

4 Place chicken in a baking dish. Bake, basting regularly for 45 minutes to 1 hour or until chicken is tender.

SERVES 4 TO 6

CHICKEN WITH SPICY LAMB STUFFING

45 g ghee
500 g lean lamb, trimmed and minced
½ cup (60 g) pine nuts
¾ cup (125 g) rice
½ teaspoon ground cinnamon
salt and freshly ground black pepper
1½ kg chicken

1 Preheat oven to 180°C (350°F).
2 Heat ghee, and sauté lamb over moderate heat until starting to change colour. Break up any lumps with a wooden spoon. Using a slotted spoon, remove meat to a bowl.
3 Add pine nuts to pan and sauté until golden. Drain and add to meat.
4 Cover rice with boiling water then pour into a strainer and rinse with cold water until water runs clear. Drain well. Add to meat. Mix in cinnamon, and salt and pepper to taste.
5 Lift up neck skin of chicken and place a little stuffing in the crop. Smooth and pull skin under the body. Place remainder of stuffing in cavity.
6 Truss chicken and place in a roasting pan. Brush with melted ghee. Cover with foil and roast for 1¼ to 1½ hours or until cooked when tested. Baste occasionally. To brown chicken, remove foil for final 20 minutes of cooking.

SERVES 4 TO 6

CHICKEN AND OKRA CASSEROLE

1½ kg chicken, jointed
2 tablespoons oil
3 onions, thinly sliced
salt and freshly ground black pepper
500 g okra, sliced
6 tomatoes, peeled, seeded and chopped
3 to 4 cups (750 ml to 1 litre) chicken stock

1 Preheat oven to 180°C (350°F).
2 Place chicken in a pan, cover with water and simmer for 25 minutes. Drain and reserve liquid.
3 Heat oil and sauté onions until transparent. Drain and place in a casserole. Top with chicken pieces and season with salt and pepper. Add okra and tomatoes and sufficient stock to half cover ingredients.
4 Cover and bake for 45 to 50 minutes or until chicken and okra are tender. Serve hot with rice.

SERVES 4

MARINATED CHICKEN ON SKEWERS

3 onions, grated
juice 3 lemons
750 g chicken thigh fillets, cut into 2 cm cubes
60 g butter or ghee, melted

1 Combine onions and lemon juice in a bowl. Add chicken and marinate for at least 2 hours.
2 Remove chicken and combine butter with marinade. Thread meat onto lightly greased skewers and cook over glowing coals for 5 minutes or until meat is tender. Baste with marinade and turn once. Serve with melted butter.

SERVES 4

✤ OKRA

Okra is believed to have originated in Abyssinia (now Ethiopia) and the east of Sudan. It is said that okra was taken to Egypt and other Ardo countries by slave-raiders. Okra are rich in various vitamins and minerals. They should be tender when bought and can be kept in the refrigerator for up to 2 weeks. They can be cooked whole or sliced and used in stews, stir-fries, soups, casseroles and salads.

Tomato Chicken Stew

salt and freshly ground black pepper

pinch cinnamon

juice ½ lemon

1½ kg chicken pieces

20 g butter

1 tablespoon olive oil

6 tomatoes, peeled, seeded and chopped

2 cups (500 ml) chicken stock

pinch sugar

1 In a bowl, combine salt and pepper, cinnamon and lemon juice. Brush chicken pieces on all sides with this mixture and leave for 10 minutes.

2 Pat chicken dry with absorbent paper (paper towels) and reserve any excess marinade.

3 Heat butter and oil in a casserole dish and sauté chicken pieces until browned on all sides. Remove from pan and keep warm.

4 Add tomatoes to pan and sauté 1 minute. Add excess marinade, stock and sugar and bring to the boil. Simmer vigorously for 7 minutes.

5 Return chicken to the pan, reduce heat, cover and simmer 45 minutes or until chicken is tender.

SERVES 4

⊹ **COUSCOUS**

Couscous is a grain made from wheat. It is finer than rice and can be substituted for rice in many recipes. It is an excellent source of iron and protein, but the iron is absorbed more efficiently if Vitamin C is consumed at the same time.

Couscous is available from supermarkets, health food stores and Middle Eastern specialty stores.

Yoghurt Marinated Duck

1½ cups (375 ml) natural yoghurt

1 teaspoon freshly ground black pepper

2 cloves garlic, crushed

4 duck breast fillets

1 tablespoon oil

1 cup (155 g) long grain rice

⅓ cup (40 g) toasted pine nuts

⅓ cup (60 g) currants

2 tablespoons chopped fresh mint

1 Place duck fillets in a bowl. Mix yoghurt, pepper and garlic and pour over duck. Leave for 3 hours or overnight.

2 Heat oil in a large frying pan. Remove duck from yoghurt marinade and cook for 2 minutes each side or until tender. Set aside and keep warm.

3 Cook rice in boiling water until tender. Drain and stir through pine nuts, currants and mint. Serve duck with rice.

SERVES 4

Chicken Couscous with Fruit and Nuts

1 tablespoon oil

4 chicken breast fillets, cut into strips

1 tablespoon honey

½ teaspoon ground cumin

1 cup (170 g) couscous

20 g butter, softened

⅓ cup (60 g) chopped hazelnuts, roasted

⅓ cup (60 g) currants or raisins

2 tablespoons chopped fresh mint

1 teaspoon freshly ground black pepper

2 teaspoons orange rind

1 Heat oil in a large frying pan. Sauté chicken for 4 minutes or until tender and golden. Add honey and cumin to pan. Set aside and keep warm.

2 Wash couscous well in cold water. Place couscous in a bowl and cover with hot water. Leave for 1 minute. Drain well and stir through butter, then stir through hazelnuts, currants, mint, pepper and orange rind. Add mixture to chicken. Stir over medium heat for 2 minutes or until heated through.

SERVES 4

STEP-BY-STEP TECHNIQUES

DUCK WITH WALNUT AND POMEGRANATE SAUCE

3 kg duck

1 teaspoon freshly ground black pepper

SAUCE

50 g butter

2 onions, finely chopped

1¼ cups (150 g) walnuts, finely chopped

1 teaspoon turmeric

1 cup (250 ml) fresh pomegranate juice or 3 tablespoons pomegranate syrup plus water to make 1 cup (250 ml)

juice 1 lemon (optional)

2 cups (500 ml) duck or chicken stock

walnut halves or pomegranate seeds and fresh dill, to garnish

Duck with Walnut and Pomegranate Sauce

1 Using poultry shears, cut duck in half through the breast. Trim back off and use to make stock. Cut breast section in half vertically (four pieces: two with legs, two with wings).

2 Wipe pieces over and season with pepper. Prick each piece several times with a skewer.

3 Preheat oven to 190°C (375°F).

4 Heat a little oil in a baking dish, add duck and brown on both sides. Drain off excess fat. Roast duck for 20 minutes. Remove and drain off fat.

5 TO PREPARE SAUCE: Heat butter in a flameproof casserole dish. Sauté onions until golden brown. Add walnuts and turmeric, stirring well, and cook for a few minutes. Add pomegranate juice or syrup, lemon juice, if desired, and stock. Bring to the boil, reduce heat and simmer, covered, for 20 minutes.

Cut the breast sections in half vertically to give four pieces.

Drain fat from the roasted duck.

6 Add duck pieces and simmer for a further 30 minutes or until duck is tender. Arrange duck on a serving plate and spoon over sauce. Garnish with walnut halves or pomegranate seeds and fresh dill. Serve hot with rice.

SERVES 4

✥ POMEGRANATES

The prophet Mohammed recommended eating pomegranate to rid the body of envy. It was the fruit given by Venus to Paris, being a symbol of fertility.

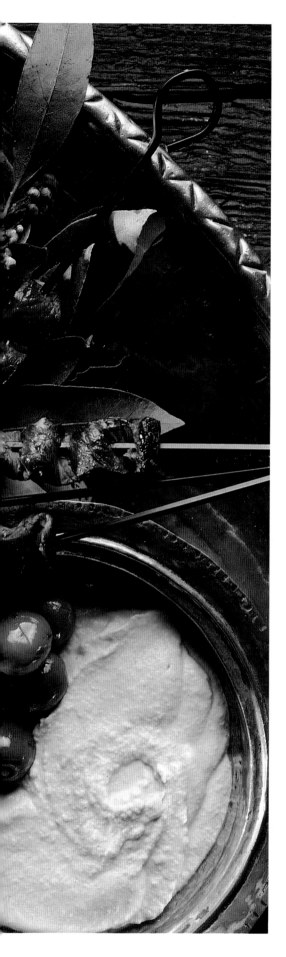

Meats

Lamb and mutton are, traditionally, the two most popular meats eaten in Greece and the Middle East. Pork is forbidden in most Middle Eastern countries for religious reasons.

Grilling is a very popular method of cooking and meats are often skewered. When cooking minced meat mixtures over coals, cook them until well browned on the outside but still pink inside: in this way they will remain moist.

Kibbeh, a favourite Lebanese and Syrian dish, can be cooked and prepared very successfully in a home kitchen. For best results, trim the meat well and take the time to mince it very finely.

Rice dishes make excellent accompaniments to meat as do vegetable and salad dishes.

This section includes recipes using lamb, beef and pork, cooked in patties, casseroles, pilafs and many more.

Lamb and Vegetable Kebabs, and Beef Kebabs

KIBBEH

1¼ kg boned leg lamb

1⅔ cups (300 g) fine burghul

1 large onion, grated

½ teaspoon ground allspice

pinch each ground cinnamon and grated nutmeg

salt

1 Trim and cut lamb into pieces and process in a food processor until almost a paste. Refrigerate.

2 Place burghul in a bowl, cover with cold water and soak for 10 minutes. Drain and press out excess moisture. Add burghul and onion to meat with spices. Salt to taste.

3 Knead for 25 minutes or process twice. Turn into bowl and knead for 10 minutes until smooth.

4 To keep mixture cold and to maintain texture, add 1 or 2 ice blocks as the mixture starts to feel warm.

MAKES 1¼ KG

BEEF KEBABS

750 g topside steak, cut into 5 mm thick, long strips

MARINADE

1½ cups (375 ml) red wine

3 cloves garlic, crushed

8 sprigs thyme, roughly chopped

2 teaspoons freshly ground black pepper

1 TO PREPARE MARINADE: Combine ingredients in a bowl. Add steak strips and marinate for 30 minutes.

2 Thread strips onto skewers. Grill for 1 to 2 minutes each side or until done. Serve on skewers with salad or remove meat from skewers and roll in flat bread (pita) spread with chick pea dip (see recipe page 18).

SERVES 6

LAMB AND VEGETABLE KEBABS

500 g lean lamb, cut into 3 cm cubes

6 baby onions, halved

12 cherry tomatoes

12 small yellow squash

12 slices zucchini (courgettes)

1 tablespoon olive oil

1 Thread lamb and vegetables alternately onto skewers. Brush lightly with olive oil. Chargrill for 2 minutes on each side.

SERVES 6

MINTED LAMB KEBABS

500 g lean lamb, cut into cubes

2 onions, cut into large cubes

2 red capsicum (peppers), cut into large cubes

6 spring onions, cut into 4 cm lengths

MARINADE

3 tablespoons chopped fresh mint

2 cloves garlic, crushed

2 tablespoons honey

½ cup (125 ml) white wine

2 tablespoons white wine vinegar

2 tablespoons oil

1 TO PREPARE MARINADE: Combine ingredients in a bowl. Add lamb, cover and marinate for at least 1 hour or overnight.

2 Thread lamb, onion, capsicum and spring onion pieces alternately onto skewers. Brush with remaining marinade and grill for 2 minutes each side or until golden brown and cooked. Serve with bread and salad.

SERVES 4

Minted Lamb Kebabs

RAW KIBBEH

½ quantity Kibbeh (see recipe page 52)

1 tablespoon olive oil

spring onions, finely chopped

1 cos lettuce, leaves separated, washed and dried

lemon wedges, to serve

1 Prepare a half quantity of kibbeh using 500 g trimmed lamb and 150 g fine burghul. Place on a platter and smooth with wet hands. Chill until serving.

2 Make an indentation in the centre with the back of a spoon and spoon in oil. Sprinkle with spring onions. Serve with lettuce leaves and lemon wedges.

SERVES 4 AS AN ENTRÉE

STUFFED KIBBEH

1 quantity Kibbeh (see recipe page 52)

1 quantity Pine Nut and Meat Stuffing (see recipe this page)

oil for deep frying

1 Divide kibbeh into 6 large or 12 small portions of even size. With wet hands, take one portion and shape into an oval. Place this in left hand and push right thumb into the centre. Rotate mixture around thumb to form a hollow. If a break occurs, reseal with a wet finger. Place a little filling in the hollow. Seal top and gently reshape the kibbeh to an oval. Repeat with remaining kibbeh and filling.

2 Heat oil for deep frying. Cook kibbeh, 2 or 4 at a time, depending on size, until a deep golden brown and cooked through. Serve hot or cold.

SERVES 6

BAKED MINCED LAMB WITH STUFFING

1 quantity Kibbeh (see recipe page 52)

3 tablespoons sesame seeds, (optional)

125 g ghee, melted

PINE NUT AND MEAT STUFFING

3 tablespoons olive oil

½ cup (60 g) pine nuts

1 onion, very finely chopped or grated

250 g lean lamb, trimmed and minced

¼ teaspoon ground allspice

pinch cinnamon

1 teaspoon freshly ground black pepper

1 Preheat oven to 190°C (375°F). Use a little of the ghee to grease a shallow rectangular baking dish or 23 cm square cake tin. Divide kibbeh mixture into three. Take one third and place it by the spoonful on base of dish. With wet hands, gently press and smooth out until it is even.

2 TO PREPARE STUFFING: Heat oil and sauté pine nuts until lightly golden. Drain and place in a bowl. Add onion to pan and sauté until soft. Add meat and cook, stirring to break up lumps, until it changes colour. Drain off excess oil. Transfer meat mixture to the bowl and add allspice, cinnamon and pepper to taste. Mix well.

3 Spread stuffing evenly over the kibbeh. Spoon remaining kibbeh over filling and, with wet hands, press and smooth out to cover.

4 With a knife, score top into diamond shapes. Dip knife into water if it becomes sticky. Pour ghee over and if desired, sprinkle with sesame seeds. Bake in the oven for 1 hour or until golden brown and crisp. Serve warm or cold.

SERVES 6

✜ GHEE

Ghee is clarified butter. It is made by heating butter until a foam forms. A milky residue then sinks to the bottom. The clarified butter can be poured off the top. It can also be purchased in supermarkets and keeps very well.

Ghee is ideal to use when sautéeing as it has a higher burning point than most oils.

From right rear clockwise: Raw Kibbeh, Stuffed Kibbeh, Baked Minced Lamb with Stuffing

*Lamb and Tomato
Rice Casserole*

LAMB AND TOMATO RICE CASSEROLE

2 tablespoons oil

1 onion, finely chopped

500 g lamb, trimmed and cubed

300 g tomatoes, peeled, seeded and chopped

3 cups (750 ml) water

½ teaspoon freshly ground black pepper

½ teaspoon ground cinnamon

1½ cups (300 g) rice

2 tablespoons chopped fresh parsley

raisins, soaked in warm water for 5 minutes

pine nuts, toasted, optional

1 Heat oil in a heavy-based pan. Sauté onion until transparent. Cook meat in batches until brown on all sides. Add tomatoes and 2 cups (500 ml) of the water. Season with pepper and cinnamon. Bring to the boil, cover and simmer for 1 hour, or until meat is tender.

2 Add rice, parsley and remaining water to pan, stirring well. Simmer covered until rice is tender. Leave pan to stand for 20 minutes before fluffing up and serving. Serve sprinkled with plumped raisins and toasted pine nuts, if desired.

SERVES 4

Minced Lamb Kebabs

pinch saffron threads

500 g lean, very finely minced lamb

1 onion, very finely chopped

2 egg yolks

pinch each ground cinnamon and cumin

salt and freshly ground black pepper

1 Soak saffron threads in 1 tablespoon boiling water and set aside to cool. Squeeze threads well.

2 Mix all ingredients well. Mix in saffron and water. Beat until light and smooth.

3 Lightly oil flat skewers and divide meat into four portions. Smooth and shape meat around skewers. Cook over hot coals or under a very hot preheated grill for 5 minutes, or until browned on the outside but still pink inside. Serve hot with rice.

SERVES 4

Lamb in Yoghurt Mint Sauce

1 tablespoon oil

1 clove garlic, crushed

½ teaspoon chilli powder

1 teaspoon paprika

8 lamb loin chops, trimmed

YOGHURT SAUCE

3 cups (750 ml) natural yoghurt

⅓ cup (40 g) plain flour

2 egg yolks

1 tablespoon chopped fresh mint

1 Preheat oven to 180°C (130°F).

2 Mix together oil, garlic, chilli and paprika. Brush mixture over chops and grill for 2 minutes each side or until tender. Place chops in an ovenproof dish.

3 TO PREPARE YOGHURT SAUCE: Place yoghurt in a bowl. Stir in flour and egg yolks and whisk until smooth. Stir in mint. Pour yoghurt sauce over chops. Bake for 15 to 20 minutes or until golden brown.

SERVES 4 TO 6

Lamb and Vegetable Hot Pot

2 tablespoons oil

1 onion, chopped

750 g lean lamb, diced

¾ teaspoon ground turmeric

1 teaspoon freshly ground black pepper

⅔ cup (160 ml) water

1 bunch English spinach

½ cup (100 g) chick peas, soaked overnight and cooked

30 g butter

1 clove garlic, crushed

½ teaspoon ground coriander

1 Heat oil in a saucepan and sauté onion until transparent. Add meat and cook, in batches, until evenly browned. Add turmeric and sauté for 20 seconds. Season with pepper and add water. Bring to the boil, reduce heat, cover and simmer for 30 minutes.

2 Remove stalks from spinach. Wash leaves, shake well and shred. Add spinach and chick peas to pan and cook for a further 20 to 30 minutes or until meat is tender. If necessary, add a little more water.

3 Just before serving, melt butter and sauté garlic and coriander for 1 minute. Pour over lamb and stir through. Serve hot with rice.

SERVES 4

GARLIC AND ROSEMARY LAMB

1 to 1½ kg leg lamb

4 cloves garlic, crushed

1 teaspoon ground rosemary

3 tablespoons fresh lemon juice

1 tablespoon honey

1 cup (250 ml) beef stock

½ cup (125 ml) dry white wine

1 Preheat oven to 180°C (350°F).

2 Place lamb on a rack in a baking dish. Make slits all over lamb with the point of a knife.

3 Mix garlic and rosemary together. Press garlic mixture into slits. Mix lemon juice and honey and brush over lamb.

Garlic and Rosemary Lamb

4 Pour stock and wine into the base of a baking dish. Bake for 1 hour 15 minutes or until lamb is tender.

Serve lamb with roast baby potatoes and pan juices.

SERVES 6

LAMB AND EGGPLANT STEW

500 g eggplant (aubergine), sliced

salt

⅓ cup (80 ml) oil

2 onions, sliced

1 kg lamb neck chops, trimmed and diced

1 teaspoon freshly ground black pepper

1½ teaspoons ground turmeric

½ teaspoon ground cinnamon

300 g tomatoes, peeled and chopped

juice ½ lemon

water

1 Sprinkle eggplant with salt, place in layers in a colander and leave for 30 minutes. Wash and pat dry with paper towels.

2 Heat half the oil in a heavy-based pan or flameproof casserole. Sauté onions until golden. Cook meat in batches until browned on all sides. Return all meat to pan. Add pepper, turmeric and cinnamon, and sauté for 30 seconds. Add tomatoes, lemon juice and enough water to just cover. Bring to the boil, reduce heat, cover and simmer over gentle heat for 1 hour.

3 Heat remaining oil and sauté eggplant until lightly coloured on both sides. Drain well and add to pan. Simmer for a further 30 minutes. Serve hot with rice.

SERVES 4

LAMB WITH DRIED FRUIT

60 g butter

1 onion, finely chopped

500 g lean lamb, diced

**⅓ cup (60 g) yellow split peas, soaked
overnight, then drained**

2 cups (500 ml) water

salt and freshly ground black pepper

⅔ cup (125 g) pitted prunes, halved

1 cup (125 g) dried apricots, quartered

½ cup (60 g) pine nuts

juice ½ lemon

1 Melt butter in a saucepan and cook onion over moderate heat until softened. Cook meat in batches until browned. Return all meat to pan with drained split peas. Add water and season to taste with salt and pepper. Bring to the boil, reduce heat and simmer, partially covered, for 30 minutes. Add more water as necessary.

2 Add prunes, apricots and nuts, and simmer for a further 15 to 20 minutes or until meat and peas are tender. Add lemon juice to taste. When the stew is quite thick, serve over rice.

SERVES 4

Lamb with Dried Fruit

SPICY MEATBALLS

90 g sliced white bread, crusts removed

500 g lean lamb, trimmed and minced twice

1 egg, beaten

1 clove garlic, crushed

½ teaspoon ground cumin

¼ teaspoon ground cinnamon

¾ teaspoon paprika

1 teaspoon freshly ground black pepper

½ cup (60 g) plain flour

45 g ghee or oil

500 g tomatoes, peeled, seeded and chopped

salt and freshly ground black pepper

1 cup (250 ml) water

1 Soak bread in water for a few minutes then squeeze dry and crumble into a bowl. Add meat to bread with egg, garlic, cumin, cinnamon, paprika and pepper. Mix very well. Take spoonfuls of mixture and, using wet hands, form into oval shapes. Roll lightly in flour.

2 Melt ghee in a pan and cook meatballs, in batches, until evenly coloured. Remove and drain.

3 Add tomatoes to pan with salt and pepper to taste, and water. Bring to the boil, reduce heat and simmer for 5 minutes.

4 Slip meatballs into sauce and simmer for 10 to 15 minutes or until cooked and tested. Serve hot with rice.

SERVES 4

PORK WITH BUTTER BEANS

1½ cups (300 g) dried butter beans

1 kg piece pork (leg or shoulder)

5 tomatoes, peeled and chopped

2 onions, sliced

1 cup (250 g) tomato purée

1 teaspoon freshly ground black pepper

1 Soak beans overnight, then drain.

2 Preheat oven to 180°C (350°F).

3 Place beans in a large saucepan, cover with water and boil for 20 to 30 minutes or until beans are almost soft. Place pork, tomatoes, onions, tomato purée, pepper and beans in baking dish. Bake for 1 hour 15 minutes or until pork is cooked.

SERVES 4 TO 6

LAMB ZUCCHINI CASSEROLE

5 tablespoons oil

750 g leg of lamb, cut into 2 cm cubes

2 onions, finely chopped

4 tomatoes peeled, seeded and chopped

2 cloves garlic, crushed

½ teaspoon salt

freshly ground black pepper

2 tablespoons finely chopped fresh parsley

2 small zucchini (courgettes), sliced

1 Heat 2 tablespoons oil in a casserole dish and sauté lamb until well browned on all sides. Add onions and sauté until softened. Stir in tomatoes, garlic, salt, pepper and parsley. Cover and simmer for 1 hour. Check from time to time to see if the mixture is becoming too dry and add stock or water, 1 tablespoon at a time, if necessary.

2 Heat remaining oil and sauté zucchini 30 minutes more. Serve from casserole dish.

SERVES 4

Lamb Zucchini Casserole

❖ BUTTER BEANS

These are also called Lima beans and have excellent nutritional value. They must be soaked overnight and then cooked for at least 10 minutes in any recipe where they are used. They are available dried and in cans and are used in soups, stews and salads.

STEP-BY-STEP TECHNIQUES

POACHED BURGHUL AND LAMB PATTIES

FILLING

45 g ghee

1 onion, very finely chopped

300 g lean lamb, trimmed and minced

½ capsicum (pepper), finely chopped

1 tablespoon each chopped fresh basil and parsley or ½ teaspoon each dried

½ teaspoon ground cinnamon

1 teaspoon freshly ground black pepper

2 tablespoons (30 g) pine nuts

LAMB PATTIES

500 g loin of lamb, trimmed and cut into pieces

1 onion, roughly chopped

1⅓ cups (250 g) fine burghul, soaked for 10 minutes

6 cups (1½ litres) chicken stock

300 g tomatoes, peeled, seeded and chopped or 2 tablespoons tomato paste (concentrated tomato purée)

1 TO PREPARE FILLING: Melt ghee in a saucepan and sauté onion for 5 minutes over moderate heat, stirring. Add meat and cook until starting to change colour, stirring to break up any lumps. Add capsicum and continue cooking until soft, about 10 minutes. Using a slotted spoon, remove meat mixture to a bowl. Add herbs, cinnamon, pepper and pine nuts to bowl. Stir to combine, then cover and cool. Refrigerate for several hours.

2 TO PREPARE LAMB PATTIES: Process lamb pieces in a food processor in batches until minced. Add onion and continue processing until mixture is very smooth in texture. Remove to a bowl.

3 Drain burghul well then press out excess water. Add meat. With wet hands, knead mixture for 15 to 20 minutes or until very well combined and smooth.

4 Take 2 tablespoons of mixture and shape into a ball with wet hands. Carefully push your thumb into the ball and work it to create a hollow centre. Place a teaspoon of chilled filling in the hollow and reseal. Reshape and flatten slightly. Repeat with remaining filling and patties.

5 Bring stock to the boil then add tomatoes and paste. Poach patties 2 or 3 at a time for 10 minutes or until cooked when tested. Drain well and keep warm.

6 Serve in bowls with a little cooking liquid and some natural yoghurt, if desired. The patties are most attractive if covered with yoghurt and sprinkled with paprika.

SERVES 6

Cook the onions, meat and capsicum in ghee, stirring frequently.

Work minced mixture into a ball, then push in thumb to form a hollow centre.

Place a teaspoon of filling in each hollow and reseal, flattening the ball slightly.

This dish is a favourite throughout both Greece and the Middle East. Zucchini (courgettes) can be used instead of or together with the eggplants. A richer flavour can be made by using a strong cheese such as Parmesan. Another popular variation in the Middle East is to pour yoghurt over the top.

MOUSSAKA

2 small eggplants (aubergines), peeled and cut into thick slices

salt

1½ tablespoons oil

60 g butter

750 g minced lamb or beef

2 onions, chopped

freshly ground black pepper

¼ teaspoon ground cinnamon

4 ripe tomatoes, peeled, seeded and chopped

3 tablespoons chopped fresh parsley

½ cup (60 g) dry breadcrumbs

60 g cheese, grated

3 egg yolks

WHITE SAUCE

40 g butter

2 tablespoons plain flour

2 cups (500 ml) milk

½ teaspoon salt

freshly ground black pepper

1 Sprinkle eggplant with salt and set aside for 15 minutes. Wash off excess salt and drain.

2 Heat oil in a frying pan. Sauté eggplant slices until lightly browned on both sides. Remove and drain on paper towels. Heat butter in the frying pan and brown the meat. Add onions and sauté until soft and golden. Season with salt and pepper to taste, and cinnamon. Add tomatoes, parsley and 2 to 3 tablespoons water. Bring to the boil and simmer for 20 minutes.

3 Sprinkle half the breadcrumbs into a buttered baking dish and cover with half the meat mixture. Add half the eggplant slices.

4 Sprinkle with one-third of the grated cheese. Repeat with layers of remaining meat, eggplant and half the remaining cheese.

5 TO PREPARE WHITE SAUCE: Melt butter, stir in flour and cook over low heat for 1 minute. Add milk gradually, stirring with a wire whisk to form a smooth medium thick sauce. Season with salt and pepper.

6 Beat egg yolks in a bowl. Add a few tablespoons of hot white sauce, then add to remaining sauce. Pour sauce over the dish, sprinkle with remaining cheese and breadcrumbs and bake for 45 minutes or until crust is crisp and brown.

SERVES 4 TO 6

LAMB WITH SPINACH, EGG AND LEMON SAUCE

½ cup (125 ml) oil

2 onions, chopped

750 g lamb, cut into 2 cm cubes

salt and freshly ground black pepper

¾ cup (180 ml) beef stock

750 g spinach, roughly chopped

2 egg yolks

2 tablespoons fresh lemon juice

1 Heat 4 tablespoons oil and sauté onions until soft and golden. Add lamb and sauté for 5 minutes over high heat.

2 Add salt and pepper to taste, and beef stock, reserving 2 tablespoons of stock. Simmer gently for 45 minutes or until meat is tender.

3 Simmer spinach in its own juice in a covered saucepan for 5 minutes or until tender. Drain and chop roughly. Season with salt and pepper to taste.

4 Spread spinach on top of the meat, drizzle with remaining oil and simmer for 15 minutes.

5 Beat egg yolks until light and creamy. Add lemon juice and reserved beef stock and pour over meat and spinach. Cook over very low heat for 10 minutes, being very careful not to let the mixture boil. Serve with rice.

SERVES 4

MEATBALLS WITH SPINACH AND CHICK PEAS

750 g minced beef or lamb

1 onion, grated

1 cup (60 g) fresh breadcrumbs

1 egg, lightly beaten

1 teaspoon ground cumin

2 tablespoons olive oil

20 g butter

1 bunch spinach, chopped

2 cloves garlic, crushed

2 cups (500 ml) beef stock

375 g canned chick peas (garbanzos), drained

2 tablespoons chopped fresh coriander

2 tablespoons cornflour blended with 1 tablespoon of water

1 Place mince, onion, breadcrumbs, egg and cumin in a bowl and mix well to combine. Shape into small balls. Heat oil in a frying pan and brown meatballs on all sides. Set aside.

2 Melt butter in the frying pan, add spinach and garlic and sauté until spinach is soft. Drain well. Return meatballs to the pan with stock. Simmer for 5 to 6 minutes.

3 Add chick peas, coriander and cornflour mixture. Stir for 2 minutes or until heated through and sauce is thick. Serve with steamed basmati rice or flat bread.

SERVES 4

VEAL WITH OLIVES

30 g butter

4 large veal steaks

4 baby onions, cut into wedges

440 g canned peeled tomatoes, crushed

3 tablespoons white wine

¼ teaspoon ground nutmeg

1 teaspoon freshly ground black pepper

12 green olives

12 black olives

4 artichoke hearts, cut into quarters

1 Melt butter in a large frying pan. Cook veal for 2 to 3 minutes each side or until tender. Set aside and keep warm.

2 Sauté onions in pan until golden. Add remaining ingredients and simmer until sauce has thickened. Return veal to pan for 1 minute, then serve.

SERVES 4

WINE POT ROAST

1 tablespoon oil

30 g butter

2 onions, chopped

3 cloves garlic, crushed

1 kg piece topside or blade steak

½ cup (125 ml) white wine

440 g canned peeled tomatoes (concentrated tomato purée)

2 tablespoons tomato paste

1 bay leaf

1 teaspoon ground oregano

1 Heat oil and butter in a large pan. Sauté onions and garlic for 2 minutes or until soft and golden. Remove from pan and set aside.

2 Brown meat in pan slowly on all sides. Add remaining ingredients and onion mixture to pan. Simmer, covered, turning meat occasionally for 1½ hours or until meat is tender. Serve with steamed seasonal vegetables and pan juices.

SERVES 6

✦ **ARTICHOKES**
Although fresh artichokes can be used in recipes, they are time-consuming to prepare. It is suggested that you use artichoke hearts packed in brine, available in cans and jars.

Vegetables & Salads

Middle Eastern and Greek cooking incorporates a large variety of vegetables. The most popular ones include eggplant (aubergine), capsicum (peppers), tomatoes, cabbage and zucchini (courgettes). These are often stuffed, stewed or made into dips and salads. Spinach is another favourite of the region, being used in soups, pies and pastries. Grains and legumes are also used widely. Chick peas and lentils feature in many Middle Eastern dishes and various beans are used in salads and vegetable recipes.

Salads should always be made with the freshest of ingredients. Herbs in particular should always be fresh for the best flavour.

Greek Country Salad and Date and Lentil Pilav

In many recipes it is necessary to salt eggplant pieces and leave for about 15 to 30 minutes, so that excess moisture and bitter juices are drawn out. Rinse the salt off then dry the slices on absorbent paper. Eggplant can be stored in the refrigerator for about 2 weeks and should not be wrapped. If it is cut, it will go brown quickly.

EGGPLANT SALAD

500 g eggplant (aubergine)

salt

3 tablespoons oil

1¼ cups (310 ml) natural yoghurt

2 cloves garlic, finely chopped

freshly ground black pepper

1 Top and tail eggplant, halve lengthways and cut into slices about 1 cm thick. Sprinkle slices with salt and set aside in a colander for 30 minutes.

2 Rinse and dry eggplant using absorbent paper or a clean tea-towel.

3 Heat oil in a frying pan. Fry slices in batches until tender. Drain and cool.

4 Spread a little yoghurt in a serving dish and cover with a layer of eggplant. Sprinkle with some garlic and pepper. Repeat layers, finishing with yoghurt. Cover and serve chilled.

SERVES 4

BEAN AND WALNUT SALAD

500 g green beans, topped and tailed

WALNUT DRESSING

1 cup (125 g) walnut pieces, finely chopped

2 cloves garlic, finely chopped

1 onion, finely chopped

3 tablespoons finely chopped fresh coriander

1½ teaspoons paprika

¼ cup (60 ml) red wine vinegar

salt and cayenne pepper

vegetable or chicken stock

1 Plunge beans into boiling water and cook uncovered for 8 to 10 minutes or until tender but still firm. Drain and refresh in cold water.

2 TO PREPARE DRESSING: In a bowl, combine walnuts, garlic, onion, coriander, paprika and vinegar. Add salt and cayenne pepper to taste. Blend well, adding sufficient stock to bring mixture to the consistency of a paste.

3 Stir dressing through beans, being careful not to bruise beans. Taste for seasoning and serve chilled.

SERVES 4

VEGETABLE AND HERB SALAD

1 lettuce, torn into pieces

1 cucumber

½ bunch radishes, thinly sliced

½ bunch spring onions, sliced

3 tablespoons finely chopped fresh parsley

3 tablespoons fresh dill, chopped

250 g tomatoes, seeded and diced

10 mint leaves shredded (optional)

125 g feta cheese, diced

DRESSING

1 clove garlic, crushed

juice 2 to 3 lemons

freshly ground black pepper

½ cup (125 ml) olive oil

1 Place lettuce in a salad bowl. Peel cucumber, leaving a little green and halve lengthways. Scoop out and discard seeds, then slice cucumber. Add it to lettuce with radishes, spring onions, parsley, dill, tomatoes and mint. Mix lightly but thoroughly. Toss through feta.

2 TO PREPARE DRESSING: Place garlic, lemon juice and pepper to taste in a small bowl. Whisk with a fork. Gradually add oil, whisking constantly. Pour over salad, toss well and serve.

SERVES 4

PEASANT SALAD

1 round Lebanese bread (pita), toasted

2 cucumbers, peeled and sliced

½ lettuce, washed and shredded

2 spring onions, chopped

½ bunch fresh parsley, finely chopped

3 tablespoons finely chopped fresh mint

red capsicum (pepper), shredded, or
cucumber, thinly sliced, to garnish

DRESSING

juice 1 lemon

½ cup (125 ml) olive oil

2 cloves garlic, crushed

freshly ground black pepper

1 Cut bread into cubes and sprinkle with a little water. Place in a bowl with cucumber, lettuce, spring onions, parsley and mint. Toss well.

2 TO PREPARE DRESSING: Place lemon juice, oil, garlic and pepper to taste in a jar and shake well. Pour dressing over salad and garnish with capsicum or cucumber.

SERVES 4

Peasant Salad

HARICOT BEAN SALAD

1½ cups (300 g) dried haricot beans, soaked
for 24 hours

2 small onions, thinly sliced

5 tablespoons chopped fresh parsley

1 red capsicum (pepper), chopped

1 hard-boiled egg, chopped

1 tomato, chopped

⅓ cup (60 g) black olives, pitted

juice 1 lemon

olive oil

Haricot Bean Salad

1 Drain beans and cook in unsalted water until tender. Cool in liquid. Drain and place in a shallow dish.

2 Cover beans with onions, parsley, capsicum, egg and tomato, and top with olives. Sprinkle over lemon juice and drizzle lightly with olive oil. Serve chilled.

SERVES 4 TO 6

GREEK COUNTRY SALAD

1 cos lettuce, broken into pieces

1 cucumber, chopped

1 green capsicum (pepper), chopped

3 tomatoes, cut into wedges

1 red onion, thinly sliced

250 g feta cheese, broken into small pieces

20 Kalamata (black) olives

1 tablespoon fresh oregano

1 tablespoon fresh mint

1 tablespoon chopped fresh parsley

DRESSING

2 tablespoons fresh lemon juice

3 tablespoons olive oil

1 teaspoon freshly ground black pepper

1 TO PREPARE SALAD: Place all ingredients in a bowl and toss well.

2 TO PREPARE DRESSING: Combine ingredients in a screwtop jar. Shake well and pour over salad. Serve with warm bread.

SERVES 4

❖ FETA CHEESE

This is available in bulk at delicatessens or packaged at supermarkets. It is packed in brine and should be stored as it is packed, but drained before use. It is used in salads and pies.

STEP-BY-STEP TECHNIQUES

Place the yoghurt in a fine sieve or piece of cheesecloth to collect the excess liquid.

Wash spinach and trim off thick stalks. Drain and roughly shred leaves.

Stir yoghurt into spinach mixture and adjust seasoning to taste.

SPINACH YOGHURT SALAD

1¼ cups (310 ml) natural yoghurt

1 kg English spinach

2 tablespoons oil

2 small onions, finely chopped

2 cloves garlic, crushed

1 teaspoon freshly ground black pepper

20 g ghee

1 teaspoon ground turmeric

1½ teaspoons dried mint

1 Place yoghurt in a piece of cheesecloth. Tie with string and suspend over a bowl to collect liquid. Leave for 2 to 3 hours until it is well drained and thick.

2 Wash spinach well and trim off thick stalks. Drain and roughly shred leaves.

3 In a large pan, heat oil and sauté onions until transparent. Stir in spinach and toss gently. Cook until liquid evaporates. Stir in garlic and sprinkle with freshly ground black pepper. Cool.

4 Place spinach mixture in a bowl and stir in yoghurt. Adjust seasoning to taste.

5 Heat ghee in a small pan and stir in turmeric and crushed mint. Place salad in a serving dish and sprinkle with flavoured ghee.

SERVES 4

Spinach Yoghurt Salad

CABBAGE SALAD

¼ large white cabbage

salt and freshly ground black pepper

2 cloves garlic, crushed

juice 2 lemons

½ cup (125 ml) olive oil

1 Shred cabbage leaves finely, discarding any hard stems; sprinkle with salt and leave for 30 minutes. Rinse well then pat dry with absorbent paper. Place in a salad bowl.

2 Combine garlic and lemon juice with pepper. Gradually whisk in oil. Pour over cabbage and toss well.

SERVES 4

✦ **TABBOULI**

There are several different methods of spelling tabbouli, among them tabbouleh, tabbuli and tabbuil. The quantities of mint, parsley, burghul, lemon juice and oil can be adjusted according to taste but plenty of parsley is the most popular preference. Tabbouli is traditionally a Lebanese dish. It is often eaten with meat or falafel wrapped up in flat bread, together with chick pea dip.

TABBOULI
Cracked Wheat Salad

1 cup (185 g) fine burghul

3 spring onions, finely chopped

1 bunch finely chopped fresh parsley

½ bunch finely chopped fresh mint

juice 2 to 3 lemons

3 tablespoons olive oil

1 teaspoon pepper

3 tomatoes, seeded and chopped

1 Place burghul in a bowl and cover with cold water. Leave to soak for 30 minutes. Drain thoroughly and press out excess water. Spread burghul on a clean, dry tea-towel and leave to dry.

2 Place burghul in a bowl with spring onions and mix well. Add parsley, mint, lemon juice, oil and pepper. Mix lightly but thoroughly.

3 Just before serving, lightly fold tomatoes into tabbouli and place the mixture on a serving dish or in lettuce leaf cups. Serve with flat bread.

SERVES 4

BROAD BEANS WITH LEMON

2½ cups (500 g) small dried broad beans (fava beans), soaked overnight

3 cloves garlic, crushed

½ cup (125 ml) olive oil

juice 2 lemons

1 teaspoon freshly ground black pepper

chopped fresh mint, to garnish

1 Drain beans, place in a large saucepan and cover with water. Bring to the boil and cook over gentle heat until tender, about 45 minutes. Stir occasionally, adding more water if necessary.

2 Drain beans and mix in garlic, oil, lemon juice and pepper. Serve hot or cold, garnished with chopped mint.

SERVES 4

RED AND GREEN CAPSICUM WITH YOGHURT

2 green capsicum (peppers)

2 red capsicum (peppers)

2 tablespoons olive oil

salt and white pepper

1 cup (250 ml) natural yoghurt

1 Halve capsicum lengthways. Remove cores and seeds and trim membranes. Place capsicum, skin side up, under a preheated grill. Grill until skin wrinkles and starts to char. Remove and cool slightly. Peel off skin.

2 Heat oil in a pan and sauté capsicum for 2 minutes on each side. Drain and place in a shallow serving dish. Season lightly with salt and pepper. Spoon yoghurt over and chill until ready to serve.

SERVES 4

Date and Lentil Pilav

DATE AND LENTIL PILAV

1⅔ cups (310 g) lentils

250 g butter

1 onion, finely chopped

1 cup (125 g) dried apricots, chopped

1½ cups (250 g) dates, seeded and chopped

½ cup (60 g) blanched almonds, chopped

½ cup (90 g) raisins

3 cups (500 g) long grain rice, cooked

1 Cook lentils in simmering water until tender, then drain.

2 Melt half the butter and combine with 1 cup (250 ml) warm water. Set aside and keep warm. Heat remaining butter and sauté onion until tender. Stir in apricots, dates, almonds and raisins. Place to one side.

3 Place half of the butter and water solution in a saucepan, cover with one-third of the rice, half the lentils, another third of the rice, dried fruits, remaining rice and lentils, and remaining butter and water. Cover pan, first with a cloth then with a lid and cook over a very low heat for 30 to 40 minutes. Serve hot on a platter.

SERVES 6

CUCUMBER WITH YOGHURT

2 cucumbers, peeled

2 cups (500 ml) natural yoghurt

salt and freshly ground black pepper

1 tablespoon chopped fresh dill

extra dill, for garnish

1 Cut cucumbers lengthways and scoop out seeds. Dice cucumber and combine with yoghurt, salt and pepper to taste, and dill.

2 Chill well and garnish with extra dill.

SERVES 2

LENTILS

Red lentils should be used in the Date and Lentil Pilav. They take about 15 to 20 minutes to cook. Brown or green lentils still have skins and are whole, and can be soaked overnight to reduce cooking time. Lentils are an excellent source of protein and other nutrients.

STUFFED CABBAGE ROLLS

1 kg cabbage

juice 1 lemon

1 clove garlic, crushed

2 teaspoons dried mint

natural yoghurt, to serve

red capsicum (pepper), cut in strips or red cabbage, shredded to garnish

STUFFING

500 g minced lean lamb

¾ cup (150 g) rice, well washed

2 cloves garlic, crushed

½ teaspoon ground cinnamon

pinch ground allspice

freshly ground black pepper

Stuffed Cabbage Rolls

1 Remove core from cabbage and separate leaves, retaining damaged ones. Set these aside for later. Blanch leaves a few at a time in boiling water. Place in a colander to drain and cool. When cool enough to handle, place leaves on a flat surface and remove hard stalk. All leaves should be of a similar size — cut large ones in half if necessary.

2 TO PREPARE STUFFING: In a bowl, combine lamb, rice, garlic, cinnamon, allspice and pepper to taste. Place small amounts of this mixture on each leaf. Fold over tops and sides and roll up.

3 Line base of a saucepan with a few damaged leaves. Layer cabbage rolls, seam-side down, in pan. Invert a saucer or small plate over rolls and add sufficient water to cover. Bring to the boil, reduce heat, cover and simmer for 45 minutes.

4 Combine lemon juice, garlic and mint in a small bowl. Carefully lift plate from cabbage rolls and add lemon juice mixture. Remove rolls and serve hot with yoghurt. Garnish with capsicum or cabbage.

SERVES 4 TO 6

BURGHUL AND LENTIL PATTIES

1 cup (200 g) brown lentils, washed and picked over

2½ cups (625 ml) water

½ cup (90 g) fine burghul

90 g butter

1 onion, finely chopped

freshly ground black pepper

1 capsicum (pepper), finely chopped

½ bunch spring onions, finely chopped

3 tablespoons very finely chopped fresh parsley

½ teaspoon paprika

1 Place lentils and water in a saucepan and bring to the boil. Reduce heat, cover and simmer for 30 to 40 minutes or until lentils are tender. Add more water if necessary.

2 Add burghul and 60 g butter and cook for a few minutes, stirring. Cover and set aside.

3 Melt remaining butter and sauté onion until transparent and golden, stirring occasionally. Cool slightly. Place onion and butter and lentil mixture in a bowl. Stir to combine and add pepper to taste. Mix well by hand for a few minutes. Add most of the capsicum, spring onions and parsley and mix well.

4 Take 3 tablespoons of mixture and, with moistened hands, form into patty shapes. Place on a serving plate and sprinkle with remaining capsicum, spring onion and parsley. To serve, dust with paprika.

SERVES 2 TO 4

CAULIFLOWER WITH AVOCADO AND TAHINI SAUCE

1 small cauliflower, broken into florets
fresh mint, to garnish

SAUCE
1 cup (250 ml) tahini, beaten
1 clove garlic, crushed with a little salt
juice 2 lemons
1 large avocado, puréed
½ bunch finely chopped fresh parsley
salt and freshly ground black pepper
vegetable stock, to thin (optional)

1 Cook cauliflower in boiling water until just tender. Refresh in cold water and drain.

2 TO PREPARE SAUCE: Blend tahini, garlic, lemon juice, avocado and parsley. Add salt and pepper to taste. The mixture should resemble very thick cream. Add a little stock if you want to thin it.

3 Pour sauce over prepared cauliflower and garnish with mint. Serve hot or cold.

SERVES 4

STUFFED QUINCES

¼ cup (45 g) yellow split peas
1½ cups (375 ml) water
4 large or 6 small quinces
40 g butter
1 onion, finely chopped
300 g minced topside steak
½ teaspoon ground cinnamon
freshly ground black pepper

SAUCE
⅔ cup (180 ml) water
juice 2 to 3 lemons
sugar

1 Bring split peas and water to the boil, reduce heat and simmer for 30 minutes or until tender. Drain.

2 Cut a slice from the top of each quince. Using an apple corer or small sharp knife carefully remove seeds and some of the flesh.

3 Preheat oven to 180°C (350°F).

4 Melt butter in a pan and sauté onion until soft. Add meat and cook for 5 minutes, stirring well to break up any lumps. Add cinnamon and sauté for a further 30 seconds. Remove from heat. Add cooked peas and season to taste with pepper.

5 Stuff quinces with the mixture.

6 Place quinces in an ovenproof container that will hold them neatly. Combine water and lemon juice with sugar to taste and pour around quinces. Bake for 45 minutes or until quinces are tender, basting occasionally. Serve hot with rice.

SERVES 4

✥ **STUFFED QUINCES**

This dish is eaten widely in Greece and Middle Eastern countries, with many variations. The Turkish version adds spices such as allspice and nutmeg, and fresh herbs such as parsley and mint, to the filling. The sauce can be varied with the addition of cinnamon sticks.

This nutritious vegetable is a favourite in Greek and Middle Eastern dishes, appearing in soups, salads, stews and casseroles. It can also be stir-fried, cooked in the microwave, baked or boiled. It's best to use fresh okra if possible, but it can be purchased in dried form or canned in brine, from specialty food stores.

OKRA WITH TOMATOES

1 kg young okra
white vinegar
½ cup (125 ml) olive oil
375 g pickling onions, peeled
3 cloves garlic, crushed
1 teaspoon ground coriander
freshly ground black pepper
500 g tomatoes, peeled and sliced
juice 1 lemon

1 Preheat oven to 180°C (350°F).
2 Scrub okra and peel off hard stems. Place on a baking sheet and sprinkle with vinegar. Place in oven for a few minutes.
3 Heat half the oil in a pan and sauté onions with garlic and coriander until soft and golden. Remove from pan. Heat remaining oil in pan and sauté okra. Season to taste with pepper and cook until slightly softened. Add tomatoes and onion mixture. Cover with water, bring to the boil and simmer for 45 minutes, or until okra is tender.
4 Sprinkle over lemon juice. Cover pan and leave for a few minutes before serving hot, or cool in pan and serve cold.

SERVES 4

BAKED VEGETABLE OMELETTE

2 leeks
1 bunch English spinach
8 eggs
salt and freshly ground black pepper
4 spring onions, finely sliced
½ lettuce, finely shredded
4 tablespoons finely chopped fresh parsley
¾ cup (90 g) walnuts, chopped
60 g butter, melted
natural yoghurt

1 Preheat oven to 170°C (330°F).
2 Trim leeks and slice lengthways, almost through to the roots. Rinse well under cold water, separating leaves to remove grit. Shake well to dry and slice thinly.
3 Wash spinach, shake well to dry and trim stalks. Chop finely.
4 Whisk eggs in a large bowl with salt and pepper to taste. Add all prepared vegetables, parsley and walnuts and combine well.
5 Grease a suitable sized shallow casserole dish with butter or melt butter in a deep-sided 20 or 23 cm cake tin. Pour in mixture and bake for 1 hour. Serve hot or cold with yoghurt.

SERVES 4

BRAISED LEEKS

1 kg leeks
2 tablespoons olive oil
3 onions, sliced
3 tomatoes, peeled and chopped
1 teaspoon freshly ground black pepper
1 cup (250 ml) vegetable stock
½ cup (125 ml) tomato purée
2 tablespoons chopped fresh oregano

1 Remove outer leaves of the leeks and cut off root end. Wash thoroughly and cut in half crossways.
2 Heat oil in a large saucepan and sauté onions slowly until light brown. Add leeks and sauté a few minutes, turning them carefully so they remain intact.
3 Add tomatoes, pepper, stock and tomato purée and bring to the boil. Reduce heat and simmer 15 minutes. Remove from heat and let leeks cool completely. Sprinkle with oregano and serve.

SERVES 4

Braised Leeks

*For this well-known
Turkish dish there are at
least two versions of the
story describing how the
recipe was named. Imams,
who were priests and
often teachers, were
reported to be mean and
bad-tempered. According
to one explanation, the
Imam's wife had spent all
day creating a new dish
from eggplant, and the
Imam thought the dish so
superb he fainted with
joy. Others say that the
Imam's wife had
created a new dish with
eggplant and, on being
told the price of the
ingredients, the Imam
fainted with shock.*

TURKISH STUFFED EGGPLANT

The Swooning Imam — Imam Bayildi

4 x 500 g eggplants (aubergines)
salt and freshly ground black pepper
1½ cups (375 ml) olive oil
4 onions, thinly sliced
4 to 6 cloves garlic, crushed
4 tomatoes, peeled and sliced
2 cups (500 ml) water
juice 1 lemon
chopped fresh parsley, to garnish

1 Trim stems from eggplants and peel, in
strips, lengthways. Make 2 lengthways slits
on tip of eggplant, in the peeled sections.
Sprinkle with salt and rub into peeled
sections; leave for 30 minutes. Rinse and dry
eggplants.

2 Heat ⅓ cup (100 ml) oil and sauté
eggplants in batches, for 5 minutes. Remove
and drain well. Sauté onions in the pan for
5 minutes. Add garlic and cook for a further
2 minutes. Remove from heat and combine
with tomatoes. Add salt and pepper to taste.
Stuff the slit of the eggplant with mixture.

3 Place eggplants in a small flameproof
baking dish or casserole that holds them
neatly. Pour over remaining oil and water
and place any remaining stuffing on top of
eggplants. Sprinkle with lemon juice. Bring
to the boil, reduce heat and simmer for
1 hour, or until tender when tested.
Serve hot, or allow to cool in liquid and
serve at room temperature or chilled.
Garnish with parsley.

SERVES 4

GREEK STUFFED EGGPLANT

2 small eggplants (aubergines)
½ cup (125 ml) olive oil
2 onions, finely chopped
2 cloves garlic, crushed
4 tomatoes, peeled and chopped
1 teaspoon salt
½ teaspoon freshly ground black pepper
½ teaspoon ground cinnamon
1 bay leaf
½ cup finely chopped fresh parsley
8 black olives
8 anchovy fillets

1 Remove stems and caps from eggplants.
Heat half the oil in a large heavy frying pan
and cook eggplants for 5 minutes. Remove
from the pan and cut in half lengthways.
Leaving a thin shell, carefully scoop out
the pulp with a spoon and chop coarsely.
Set aside.

2 Preheat oven to 200°C (400°F).

3 Heat remaining oil in the pan and sauté
onions and garlic until golden. Add
eggplant pulp, tomatoes, salt and pepper
to taste, cinnamon, bay leaf and half the
parsley. Cook slowly for 20 minutes,
stirring occasionally.

4 Fill eggplant halves with mixture and top
with olives and anchovy fillets. Bake for
10 minutes. Cool and decorate with
remaining parsley.

SERVES 2 TO 4

Stuffed eggplant

STUFFED TOMATOES WITH PINE NUTS AND HERBS

8 to 10 large tomatoes

½ cup (125 ml) olive oil

2 onions, finely chopped

¾ cup (155 g) rice

2 tablespoons currants

2 tablespoons pine nuts

2 tablespoons finely chopped fresh mint

2 tablespoons finely chopped fresh parsley

salt and freshly ground black pepper

1 Preheat oven to 180°C (350°F).

2 Cut the tops off the tomatoes and scoop out the pulp, reserving both tops and pulp.

3 Heat oil in a pan and sauté onions until browned. Stir in tomato pulp then mix in remaining ingredients. Simmer for 2 minutes then add 1¼ cups (310 ml) water and cook slowly for 7 minutes or until rice begins to soften. Season to taste.

4 Spoon mixture into tomato shells, allowing room at top for rice to swell. Replace tops and brush all over with oil. Arrange on an oiled baking tray and bake for 35 to 40 minutes.

SERVES 4 TO 5

STUFFED CAPSICUM

6 even-shaped capsicum (peppers), red or green

FILLING

1 tablespoon oil

6 spring onions, chopped

1 clove garlic, crushed

500 g minced beef or lamb

1 cup (155 g) rice, cooked

¼ cup (30 g) pine nuts

¼ cup (45 g) currants or raisins

1 tomato, peeled and chopped

½ teaspoon ground cinnamon

2 tablespoons chopped fresh parsley

¾ cup (180 ml) vegetable stock or water

1 Preheat oven to 180°C (350°F).

2 Cut tops from capsicum, remove seeds.

3 TO PREPARE FILLING: Heat oil in a large frying pan. Sauté spring onions and garlic for 1 minute. Add meat and sauté for 4 to 5 minutes or until brown. Add rice, pine nuts, currants, tomato, cinnamon and parsley. Stir well and cook for 2 minutes.

4 Spoon filling into capsicum. Place them in a large baking dish. Pour stock into base of dish. Cover with foil and bake for 30 to 35 minutes or until capsicum are soft.

SERVES 3 TO 6

TURKISH TOMATOES

8 to 10 large tomatoes

¼ cup (60 ml) olive oil

2 onions, finely chopped

2 medium-sized eggplants (aubergines), chopped

½ cup (30 g) fine fresh breadcrumbs

3 tablespoons finely chopped fresh parsley

salt and freshly ground black pepper

¾ cup (90 g) finely grated cheese

2 eggs, beaten

1 Preheat oven to 180°C (350°F).

2 Cut the tops off the tomatoes and scoop out the pulp. Reserve pulp.

3 Heat oil in a pan and sauté onions until lightly browned. Add tomato pulp and simmer for 5 minutes. Stir in eggplant and simmer for 5 minutes, or until tender. Add breadcrumbs, parsley and season to taste. Cook, stirring, for 2 minutes.

4 Remove pan from heat and beat in cheese. Stir in eggs and mix thoroughly. Spoon mixture into each tomato shell and arrange in a greased ovenproof dish. Bake for 30 minutes or until tender.

SERVES 4 TO 6

✦ **STUFFED VEGETABLES**

The fillings given in these recipes are only suggestions. Use your imagination to create your own. Try minced beef or lamb combined with various spices and onion, with or without rice. Combine meat, split peas, rice and spices. A delicious vegetarian stuffing is rice mixed with chick peas, tomatoes and spices of your choice.

CHEESE AND SPINACH PIE

Spanakopita

1 kg spinach

1 tablespoon oil

1 onion, chopped

200 g feta cheese

30 g Parmesan cheese, grated

4 eggs

2 tablespoons freshly ground black pepper

1 tablespoon chopped fresh mint

1 tablespoon chopped fresh dill

90 g butter, melted

12 sheets filo pastry

1 Preheat oven to 160°C (320°F).

2 Remove white stalks from spinach and roughly chop.

3 Heat oil in a large pan and sauté onion for 2 to 3 minutes or until golden. Add spinach and stir well for 3 to 4 minutes or until spinach is wilted. Drain spinach mixture well.

3 Mash feta in large bowl with a fork. Stir in Parmesan, eggs, pepper, mint, dill and spinach mixture.

4 Grease a deep 20 cm square cake tin with melted butter. Brush a sheet of filo pastry with butter. Ease pastry into tin to cover base and sides, with pastry overlapping rim. Repeat with 5 more sheets, placing pastry in different directions so that all of the tin is covered.

5 Pour in spinach and cheese mixture. Fold over overlapping base sheets of pastry. Brush remaining sheets of pastry, lay over top of pie, tucking ends of pastry under. Bake for 35 to 40 minutes then increase temperature to 220°C (425°F) for 5 to 10 minutes to brown top of pie. Serve hot or cold.

SERVES 4 TO 6

VEGETABLE CASSEROLE

1 large eggplant (aubergine), cut into ½ cm slices

salt

4 tablespoons olive oil

2 onions, sliced

2 green capsicum (peppers), seeded and cut into strips

2 zucchini (courgettes), sliced

250 g string beans, halved

2 cloves garlic, crushed

2 tablespoons chopped fresh parsley

½ teaspoon sugar

freshly ground black pepper

1 cup (250 ml) vegetable stock

2 tablespoons chopped fresh parsley, for garnish

1 Preheat oven to 180°C (350°F).

2 Sprinkle eggplant with salt and set aside for 15 minutes. Wash off salt, drain and pat dry with absorbent paper.

3 Heat 2 tablespoons oil in a frying pan and sauté eggplant slices on both sides until browned. Transfer to a baking dish.

4 Sauté onions and capsicum in remaining oil for 3 minutes. Add zucchini and beans and sauté for 2 more minutes, stirring frequently.

5 Place vegetables on top of eggplant. Combine garlic, parsley, sugar, pepper and stock. Pour over vegetables, cover and bake for 1 hour. Garnish with parsley and serve hot.

SERVES 4

✢ CASSEROLES

These are traditionally served with either rice, burghul or couscous. Alternatively, serve with large quantities of flat bread. For variations in the Vegetable Casserole, add chopped nuts such as hazelnuts, almonds or pine nuts, or chopped fresh herbs such as mint or coriander.

Desserts

A sweet tooth is a strong characteristic of anyone from the Middle Eastern region and the desserts and sweetmeats reflect such a craving.

All types of nuts are popular and, combined with dried fruits, make delicious and rich sweetmeats to serve with coffee. Prepare a few for each guest and serve in individual paper cases.

Dates and figs, almonds and honey are popular ingredients for desserts, many of which are delightfully rich yet not too heavy.

Coffee, Turkish or Arabian, makes a good finish to a meal.

Yoghurt Cake

ORANGE BLOSSOM PANCAKES

2 cups (250 g) self-raising flour

½ cup (125 g) caster sugar

2 cups (500 ml) water

1 teaspoon orange blossom water

1 tablespoon grated orange rind

1 teaspoon vanilla essence

icing sugar and cinnamon, for dusting

1 Place flour and sugar in a large bowl and make a well in the centre. Add water, orange blossom water, rind and vanilla. Whisk until smooth.

2 Pour tablespoons of mixture into a lightly greased pan. Swill pan to evenly spread batter. Cook on both sides until lightly golden. Repeat with remaining batter. Dust pancakes with icing sugar and cinnamon.

MAKES ABOUT 30

✥ ORANGE BLOSSOM WATER

This is mainly used to flavour syrups, drinks, desserts and other confectionery.

EASTER BREAD

⅔ cup (160 ml) milk

75 g butter

1½ tablespoons caster sugar

¼ teaspoon salt

25 g compressed yeast

2 tablespoons warm water

6 cups (750 g) plain flour

2 eggs, lightly beaten

2 teaspoons grated lemon rind

extra egg, for glazing

¼ cup (30 g) flaked almonds

1 Heat milk in a pan until almost boiling. Add butter, sugar, salt and stir until dissolved. Mix yeast and water together until smooth. Add to milk.

2 Place flour in a large bowl. Gradually add milk mixture, eggs and lemon rind. Mix to a soft dough.

✥ COMPRESSED YEAST

Always store compressed yeast in the refrigerator in a sealed jar or airtight plastic bag. It will only keep for about 2 weeks, unlike dried yeast which keeps for 1 year. Compressed yeast cannot be frozen. Two metric teaspoons of dried yeast is equivalent to 30 g fresh compressed yeast.

3 Place dough on a lightly floured board and knead until smooth and elastic, 5 to 10 minutes. Place dough in a lightly oiled bowl. Cover with a tea-towel and stand in a warm place for 15 to 20 minutes or until dough doubles in size. Knead dough for 1 minute. Divide into three portions. Roll into long pieces. Plait dough and shape into a circle. Place on a baking tray and leave to rise for 20 to 30 minutes.

4 Preheat oven to 180°C (350°F).

5 Glaze with extra egg and sprinkle with almonds. Bake for 30 minutes or until cooked. Traditionally, this Easter Bread is decorated with red easter eggs.

SERVES 6 TO 8

ALMOND PISTACHIO SWEETS

2¼ cups (250 g) ground almonds

¾ cup (125 g) icing sugar

4 to 6 tablespoons orange blossom water

¾ cup (125 g) pistachio nuts, peeled and finely chopped

3 tablespoons caster sugar

¾ cup (125 g) icing sugar, extra

¾ cup (125 g) pistachio nuts, peeled, extra

1 Combine ground almonds and icing sugar with enough orange blossom water to form a stiff paste. Knead until smooth and leave to rest.

2 Combine pistachio nuts and caster sugar.

3 Shape almond paste into small balls the size of a walnut. Using a teaspoon handle, make a small hole in each ball and fill it with pistachio sugar mixture. Close hole over filling and reshape. Roll balls in icing sugar. Decorate the top of each ball with a peeled pistachio nut. Serve with coffee.

MAKES ABOUT 40

HONEY PIE

3 cups (375 g) plain flour

¾ teaspoon salt

1½ teaspoons baking powder

100 g butter

½ cup (125 ml) cold water

3 cups (750 g) cottage cheese

¾ cup (185 g) sugar

1 teaspoon ground cinnamon

1 cup (250 ml) honey

5 eggs

icing sugar and cinnamon, for dusting

1 Preheat oven to 150°C (300°F).

2 Sift flour, salt and baking powder into a bowl. Rub in butter with fingertips until mixture is crumbly. Stir in water gradually, using only enough to make the dough stick together. Roll out pastry and press into a 27 cm pie plate.

3 Beat cottage cheese and sugar until well combined and fluffy. Add cinnamon and honey. Add eggs, one at a time, beating well after each addition. Pour mixture into pastry shell. Bake for 40 minutes. Raise oven heat to 190°C (375°F) and bake an additional 10 to 15 minutes. Turn off heat and leave the pie in the oven until completely cooled. Sprinkle with icing sugar and cinnamon.

SERVES 6 TO 8

Honey Pie

FILO PASTRY WITH HONEY AND NUTS

500 g filo pastry, cut into very thin shreds

250 g unsalted butter, melted and cooled

1½ cups (185 g) finely chopped walnuts

¾ cup (90 g) finely chopped almonds

¼ cup (60 g) sugar

1 teaspoon cinnamon

HONEY SYRUP

1 cup (220 g) sugar

1 cup (250 ml) water

2 teaspoons fresh lemon juice

½ cup (125 ml) honey

1 Preheat oven to 180°C (350°F).

2 Combine shredded filo and butter in a bowl. Toss well to coat the shreds thoroughly. Spread half into a 27 cm square baking dish.

3 Mix together nuts, sugar and cinnamon. Sprinkle evenly over pastry and top with remaining pastry. Press lightly.

4 Cover with foil and bake for 30 minutes.

5 Remove the foil and cook for a further 15 minutes or until golden brown.

6 **TO PREPARE SYRUP:** Combine sugar, water and lemon juice in a saucepan. Bring to the boil, stirring until sugar dissolves. Reduce heat and simmer until syrupy. Stir in honey until smooth.

7 Remove pastry from the oven and pour on syrup. Let cool completely. Cut into diagonal squares and serve.

SERVES 6

✥ **SHREDDED FILO**

Filo pastry can be shredded and used in place of konafa pastry.

Filo Pastry with Honey and Nuts

CREAMY SHREDDED PASTRY

SYRUP

2 cups (400 g) sugar

1½ cups (375 ml) water

juice ½ lemon

2 tablespoons orange blossom water

CREAM FILLING

2 tablespoons rice flour

1 to 2 tablespoons sugar

2 cups (500 ml) milk

1¼ cups (310 ml) cream

PASTRY

500 g konafa pastry

250 g ghee

1 **TO PREPARE SYRUP:** Combine sugar, water and lemon juice in a saucepan. Bring to the boil, stirring until sugar dissolves. Reduce heat and simmer until syrupy. Flavour with orange blossom water, cool and chill slightly.

2 Preheat oven to 190°C (375°F).

3 **TO PREPARE CREAM FILLING:** Mix rice flour and sugar in a bowl. Add half the milk and mix to a smooth paste. Bring remaining milk to the boil and pour over paste, stirring vigorously. Return mixture to saucepan and bring to the boil, stirring constantly. Cool, stir in cream thoroughly.

4 **TO PREPARE PASTRY:** Place konafa pastry in a large tray. Pull out and separate strands as much as possible. Pour over melted ghee and work with fingers until shreds are coated.

5 Place half the pastry in a small baking dish. Spread over filling and cover with remaining pastry, flattening it with the palm of your hand.

6 Bake for 45 minutes. Increase temperature to 250°C (500°F) for 10 minutes or until pastry is a light golden colour. Remove from oven and immediately pour over cold syrup. Serve hot or cold.

SERVES 6 TO 8

✥ **KONAFA PASTRY**

This shredded pastry can be bought at Greek specialty stores. It is also called kataifi by Greeks and Turks. Before using, it should be turned out into a dish and separated, then coated with ghee. Store it as you would filo pastry.

Step-by-Step Techniques

Date Pastries

In the Middle East, these pastries are made as an Easter specialty.

1⅓ cups (200 g) pitted fresh dates, roughly chopped

3 tablespoons water

2 cups (250 g) plain flour

125 g butter, chilled

2 teaspoons flavoured water, either orange blossom or rose

2 tablespoons water

icing sugar

1 Preheat oven to 180°C (350°F).

2 Combine dates and water in a small pan. Cook over gentle heat until softened. Set aside to cool.

3 Sift flour into a bowl. Cut butter into small pieces and rub into flour until mixture resembles breadcrumbs. Combine orange blossom or rose water and 2 tablespoons water and sprinkle over flour. Mix into flour using a round-bladed knife. Turn dough onto a lightly floured surface and knead for a few minutes, until soft and smooth. Cover and rest.

4 Take a spoonful of dough and shape into a round. Make a hollow with your finger and spoon in a little date stuffing. Reclose hole

Date Pastries

and reshape into a round. Decorate top lightly with a fork. Continue until dough runs out. Place on a greased baking sheet and bake for 20 to 25 minutes. If pastries start to brown, cover with foil or greaseproof paper. Remove and cool on wire racks until firm. Roll in sifted icing sugar.

MAKES ABOUT 12

Rub small pieces of butter into sifted flour until mixture resembles breadcrumbs.

Using a round-bladed knife, mix flavoured water into flour.

Spoon a little date stuffing into each round of dough.

Semolina Halva

1½ cups (375 g) sugar

2 cups (500 ml) water

110 g unsalted butter

¾ cup (125 g) semolina

1¼ cups (125 g) almonds, peeled and roughly chopped

ground cinnamon, for dusting

1 Combine sugar and water in a small saucepan. Cook over gentle heat, stirring until sugar dissolves. Simmer for 10 minutes.
2 In another pan, heat butter over a low heat until bubbling. Add semolina, stir with a wooden spoon and cook slowly until semolina is golden brown. Add syrup, stirring until well blended. Reduce heat to low, cover with greased wax paper and leave for 15 minutes. The semolina should absorb all the syrup.
3 Place mixture in a lightly greased mould, press down firmly and leave until cold. Turn out and serve, garnished with almonds and sprinkled with cinnamon.

SERVES 4

Turkish Delight

2½ cups (625 ml) water

4 cups (1 kg) sugar

1 cup (125 g) cornflour

1 cup (250 ml) fresh orange or grape juice

1 teaspoon cream of tartar

orange blossom water

red food colouring

icing sugar, for tossing

1 Bring water to the boil in a saucepan, add sugar and stir until thoroughly dissolved.
2 Blend cornflour with fruit juice and cream of tartar. Remove syrup from heat and gradually add blended cornflour. Return to heat, stirring until mixture boils. Reduce heat and cook very slowly for 20 minutes.

3 Flavour with orange blossom water, colour with a few drops of red food colouring and pour into a lightly oiled tray. When cool and set, cut into 2 cm squares and toss in icing sugar.

MAKES ABOUT 25 PIECES

Quince Paste

1 kg fresh quinces, washed

granulated sugar

caster sugar, for tossing

1 Place whole quinces in a saucepan with just enough water to cover. Bring to the boil, reduce heat and cook gently for 45 minutes or until soft when tested. Remove cores, mash and purée.
2 Measure purée in a cup measure and combine with an equal amount of sugar in a saucepan. Cook over moderate heat, stirring constantly for 20 minutes or until mixture is thick and comes away from sides of pan. Regulate heat carefully to prevent scorching.
3 Spread mixture into a wet, shallow pan and leave to set overnight. When set, cut into squares, toss in caster sugar and leave to dry on a cake cooler. When dry, wrap in waxed paper and store in a cool place. Serve with coffee.

MAKES ABOUT 1 KG

Date Halva

3 cups (500 g) fresh dates, chopped

4 cups (500 g) walnuts, chopped

finely grated rind 1 lemon

pine nuts, to garnish (optional)

1 Knead dates and walnuts together with lemon rind. Press into a slab tin. Cut into squares, decorate each square with a pine nut if desired, and serve.

MAKES ABOUT 20 PIECES

⊹ QUINCE PASTE

Take care when cooking this paste — it has a tendency to form large bubbles and spatter, so use a long-handled wooden spoon for stirring the boiling mixture. Quinces, when cooked in sugar, turn a beautiful purple colour, making this paste both attractive and delicious to eat. It is also excellent served with a cheese platter.

FIGS IN BRANDY SYRUP

½ cup (90 g) brown sugar

½ cup (125 ml) brandy

½ cup (125 ml) apple juice

1 vanilla bean

1 cinnamon stick

6 figs, quartered

cream or natural yoghurt, to serve

1 Place brown sugar, brandy and apple juice in a saucepan. Stir to dissolve sugar. Bring to the boil and simmer for 5 minutes.

2 Add vanilla bean and cinnamon stick and simmer for 2 minutes. Add figs and gently simmer for 3 to 4 minutes. Serve with cream or yoghurt.

SERVES 2 TO 4

ORANGE ICE

2 cups (500 ml) fresh orange juice

½ cup (125 ml) fresh lemon juice

1½ cups (375 g) sugar

3¼ cups (800 ml) water

1 tablespoon orange blossom water

1 Combine orange and lemon juices. Place sugar and water in a saucepan, bring to the boil, simmer for 5 minutes and cool.

2 Stir in fruit juices and orange blossom water. Pour into refrigerator trays, cover with foil and freeze. As ice freezes a little, beat lightly with a fork to reduce crystal size. Repeat at 30 minute intervals. Transfer from freezer to refrigerator 20 minutes before serving.

SERVES 4

Figs in Brandy Syrup

Step-by-Step Techniques

Baklava

Filling

1 cup (125 g) walnuts, finely chopped

1 cup (125 g) almonds, finely chopped

2 tablespoons sugar

1 teaspoon ground cinnamon

Pastry

30 sheets filo pastry

125 g ghee, melted

Syrup

1 cup (250 g) sugar

¾ cup (180 ml) water

1 tablespoon fresh lemon juice

1 Preheat oven to 230°C (450°F).

2 To Prepare Filling: Combine all ingredients in a small bowl and set aside.

3 To Prepare Pastry: Line a greased shallow-sided 23 cm square tin with 10 sheets of filo pastry, brushing each sheet with ghee. Sprinkle half nut mixture evenly over pastry. Top with another 10 sheets of filo, brushing each with ghee. Sprinkle over remaining nut mixture and cover with the last 10 sheets of filo, brushing each with ghee. With a sharp knife, cut pastry in vertical lines 6 cm apart, then cut diagonally into diamond shapes.

Baklava

4 Bake for 10 minutes then reduce oven to 190°C (375°F) for 25 minutes or until golden, crisp and baked through.

5 To Prepare Syrup: Combine sugar, water and lemon juice in a pan. Bring to the boil, stirring constantly then reduce heat. Simmer for 20 minutes without stirring.

6 When baklava is cooked, leave for a few minutes and spoon cooled syrup evenly over pastry. Cool before serving.

Makes about 20 pieces

Brush each sheet of filo pastry with melted ghee.

Sprinkle half the nut mixture evenly over first 10 layers of pastry.

Using a sharp knife, cut diagonally to make diamond shapes on pastry.

This fragrant spice is used in Greek and Middle Eastern cooking to flavour cakes and pastries and can be bought in Greek and Middle Eastern specialty stores. It comes from the kernels of a wild black cherry, first grown in Syria. The kernels were originally used in the Middle East for medicine.

It is always sold as whole seeds and these should be stored in a sealed jar in a cool, dark place.

The seeds should be ground to a powder just before using, for the best flavour.

COFFEE ROLLS

30 g compressed yeast

3 tablespoons warm water

1¼ to 1½ cups (300 to 350 ml) warm milk

2 eggs, beaten

200 g butter, melted

3 tablespoons sugar

1 teaspoon salt

**1½ teaspoons ground mahlab
or ground aniseed**

6¼ cups (800 g) plain flour

1 egg, beaten, to glaze

1 Crumble yeast into a small bowl and stir in warm water. Leave in a warm place for 5 minutes.

2 In a bowl, combine milk, eggs, melted butter, sugar, salt and mahlab or aniseed, beating well. Stir into yeast mixture.

3 Gradually add flour to liquid until a soft dough is formed. Turn out onto a lightly floured board and knead for 5 minutes or until smooth and elastic. Place dough in a lightly oiled bowl, cover with a tea-towel and leave in a warm position for about 2 hours, or until doubled in bulk (longer time is necessary to prove a yeast dough when there is such a high butter content).

4 Punch down dough, knead lightly and divide into 32 equal portions. Form into snail shapes: roll each piece of dough into a rope and, beginning at one end, wind rope around itself into a snail-shaped circle. Place on a greased tray, cover and leave to rise in a warm place for 45 minutes. Brush tops of rolls with beaten egg.

5 Preheat oven to 200°C (400°F).

6 Bake for 15 minutes or until a rich golden brown. These rolls can be frozen and reheated as necessary.

MAKES 32

ORANGE CARAMEL CUSTARD

8 egg yolks

4 tablespoons caster sugar

pinch salt

3¼ cups (800 ml) milk, heated

vanilla essence

6 oranges, peeled and thinly sliced

1 cup (225 g) sugar

2 tablespoons hot water

1 Beat egg yolks and sugar lightly in the top of a double boiler. Add salt and milk, stirring continuously. Place over hot water and stir until custard thickens. Remove pan from heat and place over cold water to cool custard. Flavour with vanilla essence.

2 Arrange orange slices in a shallow glass dish; when custard is cold, pour it over. In a heavy pan, heat sugar until melted but not browned. Slowly add hot water. Stir and cook for a minute then pour over top of custard.

SERVES 4 TO 6

YOGHURT CAKE

125 g butter

1 cup (250 g) sugar

1 cup (250 ml) natural yoghurt

2 eggs

1 tablespoon fresh lemon juice

1 tablespoon lemon rind

2½ cups (310 g) self-raising flour, sifted

½ teaspoon bicarbonate of soda

icing sugar, optional

natural yoghurt, to serve

1 Preheat oven to 180°C (350°F). Grease and line a 23 cm spring-form cake tin.

2 Cream butter and sugar in a bowl until light. Beat in yoghurt. Beat in eggs, one at a time. Add lemon juice and rind. Stir in flour and bicarbonate of soda.

3 Pour into cake tin and bake for 45 minutes, or until golden brown and firm to touch. Cool. Decorate with icing sugar if desired. Serve with whipped yoghurt.

SERVES 6 TO 8

SWEET BONNETS

5 egg yolks

pinch salt

3 tablespoons caster sugar

1 tablespoon brandy

3 tablespoons natural yoghurt

4 cups (500 g) self-raising flour, sifted

oil for deep frying

icing sugar, for dusting

1 Beat egg yolks and salt in a bowl until thick and lemon coloured. Add sugar and brandy. Beat in yoghurt. Stir in flour, working by hand into a dough.

2 Knead dough on a floured board until dough blisters, then roll out as thinly as possible. Cut into ribbons about 2½ cm wide, then divide into 7½ cm strips. Make a 2½ cm slit down the centre of each strip and pull one end through.

3 Fry in heated oil until pastries are puffed and just golden, turning once. Drain on absorbent paper and sprinkle with sifted icing sugar.

MAKES ABOUT 30

Sweet Bonnets

MEASURING MADE EASY

HOW TO MEASURE LIQUIDS

METRIC	IMPERIAL	CUPS
30 ml	1 fluid ounce	1 tablespoon plus 2 teaspoons
60 ml	2 fluid ounces	¼ cup
90 ml	3 fluid ounces	
125 ml	4 fluid ounces	½ cup
150 ml	5 fluid ounces	
170 ml	5½ fluid ounces	
180 ml	6 fluid ounces	¾ cup
220 ml	7 fluid ounces	
250 ml	8 fluid ounces	1 cup
500 ml	16 fluid ounces	2 cups
600 ml	20 fluid ounces (1 pint)	2½ cups
1 litre	1¾ pints	

HOW TO MEASURE DRY INGREDIENTS

15 g	½ oz	
30 g	1 oz	
60 g	2 oz	
90 g	3 oz	
125 g	4 oz	(¼ lb)
155 g	5 oz	
185 g	6 oz	
220 g	7 oz	
250 g	8 oz	(½ lb)
280 g	9 oz	
315 g	10 oz	
345 g	11 oz	
375 g	12 oz	(¾ lb)
410 g	13 oz	
440 g	14 oz	
470 g	15 oz	
500 g	16 oz	(1 lb)
750 g	24 oz	(1½ lb)
1 kg	32 oz	(2 lb)

QUICK CONVERSIONS

5 mm	¼ inch	
1 cm	½ inch	
2 cm	¾ inch	
2½ cm	1 inch	
5 cm	2 inches	
6 cm	2½ inches	
8 cm	3 inches	
10 cm	4 inches	
12 cm	5 inches	
15 cm	6 inches	
18 cm	7 inches	
20 cm	8 inches	
23 cm	9 inches	
25 cm	10 inches	
28 cm	11 inches	
30 cm	12 inches	(1 foot)
46 cm	18 inches	
50 cm	20 inches	
61 cm	24 inches	(2 feet)
77 cm	30 inches	

NOTE: We developed the recipes in this book in Australia where the tablespoon measure is 20 ml. In many other countries the tablespoon is 15 ml. For most recipes this difference will not be noticeable.

However, for recipes using baking powder, gelatine, bicarbonate of soda, small amounts of flour and cornflour, we suggest you add an extra teaspoon for each tablespoon specified.

USING CUPS AND SPOONS

All cup and spoon measurements are level

METRIC CUP			METRIC SPOONS	
¼ cup	60 ml	2 fluid ounces	¼ teaspoon	1.25 ml
⅓ cup	80 ml	2½ fluid ounces	½ teaspoon	2.5 ml
½ cup	125 ml	4 fluid ounces	1 teaspoon	5 ml
1 cup	250 ml	8 fluid ounces	1 tablespoon	20 ml

OVEN TEMPERATURES

TEMPERATURES	CELSIUS (°C)	FAHRENHEIT (°F)	GAS MARK
Very slow	120	250	½
Slow	150	300	2
Moderately slow	160-180	325-350	3-4
Moderate	190-200	375-400	5-6
Moderately hot	220-230	425-450	7
Hot	250-260	475-500	8-9

INDEX